PRAYER SERVICES
FOR
PARISH LIFE

JERRY GALIPEAU

017264

WORLD LIBRARY PUBLICATIONS
The Music and Liturgy Division of J. S. Paluch Company, Inc.
3825 North Willow Road • Schiller Park, Illinois 60176–2353
800 566-6150 • www.wlpmusic.com

PRAYER SERVICES FOR PARISH LIFE

WLP 017264

ISBN
1-58459-193-5

Author, Compiler, and Editor: Jerry Galipeau
Copy Editor and Contributor: Marcia T. Lucey
Typesetting and Design: Tejal Patel
Copyright © 2004 World Library Publications
3825 North Willow Road
Schiller Park, Illinois 60176-2353

TABLE OF CONTENTS

INTRODUCTION

Prayer Services for Parish Life is designed to assist priests, deacons, and parish leaders in their efforts to place parish meetings and events in the context of prayer. Most services in this book include proclamations from the sacred scriptures. Leaders may wish to assign these readings to those who are capable of good proclamation.

The first section of the book contains the texts for use by the leader. The second section contains the pages that can be duplicated for participants. The purchaser may photocopy these pages free of charge. The leader's pages could be three-hole punched and placed in an attractive binder. An added feature is the CD-ROM, found on the inside back cover, which contains all of the texts found in this book in easily downloadable format. After downloading, the user is encouraged to create as many copies of the texts as needed. More information on accessing the materials on the CD-ROM can be found on the last page of this resource.

Several penitential services are contained in *Prayer Services for Parish Life*. These were designed to be non-sacramental in nature. The *Rite of Christian Initiation of Adults* and the *Rite of Penance* suggest that these non-sacramental rites be celebrated with those preparing for initiation, as well as with all who wish to celebrate God's reconciling love. These penitential services can easily be adapted to include sacramental confession and absolution.

Since music resources vary from parish to parish, a list of music suggestions for each prayer service is included in this book. The suggestions represent music from each of the major Catholic music publishers.

We hope that *Prayer Services for Parish Life* adds to the richness of the spiritual life of your parish.

Jerry Galipeau

MUSIC SUGGESTIONS

PARISH MINISTRIES

Prayer Service for Parish Lectors
Praise to You, O Christ, Our Savior (OCP)
God Has Spoken by the Prophets
The Word Is in Your Heart (GIA)

Prayer Service for Ministers of Hospitality
All Are Welcome (GIA)
Whatsoever You Do
The Servant Song

Prayer Service for Ministers of Care
Whatsoever You Do
I Heard the Voice of Jesus Say
Come to Me

Prayer Service for Extraordinary Ministers of Communion
Taste and See
Let Us Be Bread (GIA)
One Bread, One Body

Prayer Service for Music Ministers
How Can I Keep from Singing
When in Our Music God Is Glorified
Moved by the Gospel, Let Us Move (GIA)

Prayer Service for Altar Servers
See Us, Lord, about Your Altar
Whatsoever You Do
How Lovely Is Your Dwelling Place

Prayer Service for a Meeting of the Liturgy Committee
One Bread, One Body
O Breathe on Me, O Breath of God
God, Whose Purpose Is to Kindle (GIA)

PARISH ACTIVITIES

Prayer Service for Volunteer Appreciation
We Are Called (GIA)
We Are the Light of the World
Now Thank We All Our God

Prayer Service to Welcome New Parishioners
All Are Welcome (GIA)
Now Thank We All Our God
Sing a New Song to the Lord

Prayer for a Parish Meeting
We Are Called (GIA)
Christ, Be Our Light (OCP)
Make Us One (WLP)

Parish Picnic
All Creatures of Our God and King
Now Thank We All Our God
Praise God from Whom All Blessings Flow

Prayer Before a Parish Trip
Christ Be beside Me
Christ, Be Near at Either Hand (WLP)
Companions on the Journey (OCP)

Celebrating the Gift of God's Creation
America the Beautiful
For the Beauty of the Earth
The Works of the Lord Are Created in Wisdom

PENITENTIAL SERVICES

Advent Penitential Service
Come, O Long-awaited Savior
On That Holy Mountain (WLP)
People, Look East

Lenten Penitential Service
This Is Our Accepted Time
From Ashes to the Living Font (WLP)
Draw Near, O Lord/Attende Domine
These Forty Days of Lent
Deep Within (GIA)

Penitential Service: Hope
Lord of All Hopefulness
O God, Our Help in Ages Past
The King of Love

Penitential Service: A New Beginning
I Want to Walk as a Child of the Light
Sing a New Song to the Lord
God of Day and God of Darkness (GIA)

Penitential Service: Respect for Life
For the Beauty of the Earth
Choose Life (WLP)
Hosea (Come Back to Me)

THE SACRAMENTS

Prayer Service for Baptism Preparation Sessions
Now Thank We All Our God
Spirit, Move upon the Waters (WLP)
Baptized in Water

Prayer Service for Engaged Couples Preparing for Marriage
We Have Been Told (GIA)
Love Divine, All Loves Excelling
The Greatest Gift (WLP)
When Love Is Found

THE CHRISTIAN YEAR

Prayer Service for Christian Unity
Where Charity and Love Prevail (WLP)
We Are Many Parts (GIA)
In Christ There Is No East or West

Lenten Service Based on the Final Words of Christ
Were You There
We Acclaim the Cross of Jesus (WLP)
What Wondrous Love

Blessing of Foods at Easter
At the Lamb's High Feast
Now Thank We All Our God
The Works of the Lord Are Created in Wisdom

Crowning an Image of the Blessed Virgin Mary
Hail, Holy Queen
Hail Mary, Gentle Woman
The Hail Mary (WLP)

Blessing of Pets
All Creatures of Our God and King
Sing Out, Earth and Skies (GIA)
Now Thank We All Our God

A Vigil Service Before Christmas
Lo, How a Rose E'er Blooming
People, Look East
O Come, O Come, Emmanuel
O Little Town of Bethlehem
Silent Night
O Come, Little Children

THE CIVIC YEAR

Prayer Service Before Elections
America the Beautiful
O Lord, Hear My Prayer (GIA)
Lead Me, Guide Me

Prayer Service for Independence Day
America the Beautiful
God of Our Fathers
The Star-Spangled Banner

PEACE AND COMFORT

Prayer Service for Peace Based on the Words of Saint Francis of Assisi
Let There Be Peace on Earth
Peace for Our Times (WLP)
O God of Love, O King of Peace

Service of Prayer for Peace
Let There Be Peace on Earth
Peace for Our Times (WLP)
Prayer of Saint Francis

Prayer Service for Comfort in Time of Disaster
Bring Peace to Earth Again (WLP)
Let There Be Peace On Earth
All Will Be Well (WLP)
If God Is for Us (OCP)

PRAYER SERVICE FOR PARISH LECTORS

Before the service, the Lectionary should be enthroned in a place surrounded by flowers and candles.

The leader invites all to rise.

The prayer service may begin with an appropriate song.

CALL TO WORSHIP

Leader: **May the word of God be on our lips.**

All: May the word of God be in our minds and hearts.

OPENING PRAYER

Leader: **Let us pray.**
God of the covenant,
you sent your Son into the world
to be your living word.
Strengthen us in our ministry
to bring that living word to your people.
Help us to improve our skills
so that your saving action will resound through us.
We ask this in the name of your Son, our Lord Jesus Christ,
the word made flesh who dwells among us.
He is Lord forever and ever.

All: **Amen.**

The leader invites all to be seated.

READING OF THE WORD OF GOD

First Reading
Isaiah 55:10–11

The LORD says:
For as the rain and the snow come down from heaven,
    and do not return there until they have watered the earth,
making it bring forth and sprout,
    giving seed to the sower and bread to the eater,
so shall my word be that goes out from my mouth;
    it shall not return to me empty,
but it shall accomplish that which I purpose,
    and succeed in the thing for which I sent it.
The word of the Lord.

Response

R/. See John 6:63c; Psalm 19:7, 8, 9, 10, 11

Leader: **Your words, Lord, are spirit and life.**

All: Your words, Lord, are spirit and life.

Leader: **The law of the LORD is perfect,**
reviving the soul;
the decrees of the LORD are sure,
making wise the simple.

All: Your words, Lord, are spirit and life.

Leader: **The precepts of the LORD are right,**
rejoicing the heart;
the commandment of the LORD is clear,
enlightening the eyes.

All: Your words, Lord, are spirit and life.

Leader: **The fear of the LORD is pure,**
enduring forever;
the ordinances of the LORD are true
and righteous altogether.

All: Your words, Lord, are spirit and life.

Leader: **More to be desired are they than gold,**
even much fine gold;
sweeter also than honey,
and drippings of the honeycomb.

All: Your words, Lord, are spirit and life.

Second Reading

1 John 1:1–4

We declare to you what was from the beginning, what we have heard, what we have seen with our eyes, what we have looked at and touched with our hands, concerning the word of life—this life was revealed, and we have seen it and testify to it, and declare to you the eternal life that was with the Father and was revealed to us—we declare to you what we have seen and heard so that you also may have fellowship with us; and truly our fellowship is with the Father and with his Son Jesus Christ. We are writing these things so that our joy may be complete.

The word of the Lord.

RECOMMITMENT TO THE MINISTRY OF THE WORD

The leader invites all to rise.

Leader: Brothers and sisters, Saint John speaks of God's word as the word of life. It can be seen, touched, and heard. It has the potential to bring salvation to those who hear it spoken from our mouths. As a sign of our dedication to the ministry of the word, I invite you now to come forward and reverence the word of God by placing your hands upon the Lectionary. Your response to this sign of reverence will be the words, "May I be a vessel of the word of life."

As each lector comes forward, the leader holds the Lectionary open, with its pages facing the lector. As the lector touches the open Lectionary, the leader says:

Embrace the living word of God.

Lector: May I be a vessel of the word of life.

At the conclusion of this sign of reverence, all may join in singing a familiar Gospel acclamation.

Gospel
Luke 24:44–48

Jesus said to his disciples, "These are my words that I spoke to you while I was still with you—that everything written about me in the law of Moses, the prophets, and the psalms must be fulfilled." Then he opened their minds to understand the scriptures, and he said to them, "Thus it is written, that the Messiah is to suffer and to rise from the dead on the third day, and that repentance and forgiveness of sins is to be proclaimed in his name to all nations, beginning from Jerusalem. You are witnesses of these things."

The Gospel of the Lord.

The leader invites all to be seated.

Leader: Let us spend an extended period of time in silence, reflecting on God's word, asking that God inspire us in our ministry of proclamation.

EXTENDED PERIOD OF SILENCE

INTERCESSIONS

The leader invites all to rise.

Leader: My friends, let us now pray that God's word of life will be planted deep within our hearts.

That we will continue to proclaim God's holy word, which is living and effective, we pray to the Lord.

That we will continue to sharpen our skills, proclaiming God's living word clearly and with conviction, we pray to the Lord.

That through our ministry God will soften hearts hardened by years of complacency, we pray to the Lord.

That those who have not yet heard God's saving word will be drawn into communion with the word made flesh, we pray to the Lord.

That all who proclaim God's word will grow closer to the Lord Jesus, we pray to the Lord.

Leader: Let us gather all our prayers into one by praying in the words that Jesus taught us. Our Father . . .

BLESSING AND DISMISSAL

Leader: Brothers and sisters, let us ask God to bless us. Please respond "Amen" to each blessing prayer.

May God bless us in our ministry to bring healing and strength to our community through the proclamation of the word. R/. Amen.

May the Holy Spirit, the giver of life, fill us with strength as we fulfill the ministry entrusted to us. R/. Amen.

May the Lord Jesus, the word made flesh who dwells among us, inspire us to imitate his life and works. R/. Amen.

Leader: We have been renewed and refreshed by God's holy word. Let us conclude this prayer service by offering one another a sign of Christ's peace.

The prayer service may conclude with an appropriate song.

Prayer Service for Ministers of Hospitality

The leader invites all to rise.

The prayer service may begin with an appropriate song.

Leader: Friends, the Lord promises that where two or three are gathered in his name, he is in their midst. We welcome the presence of the Lord in this place and ask that we be strengthened in our ministry to offer Christian hospitality to all who seek the living God.

Opening Prayer

Leader: Let us pray.
God of life,
you gather us together to be a sign of welcome
to all who come to praise your holy name.
Help us recognize your presence in every person
who enters our church.
Strengthen us in our dedication to show hospitality to all.
We ask this in the name of your Son,
the one who welcomed sinners into his saving presence.
He is Lord forever and ever.

All: Amen.

The leader invites all to be seated.

Reading of the Word of God

Genesis 18:1–8

The LORD appeared to Abraham by the oaks of Mamre, as he sat at the entrance of his tent in the heat of the day. He looked up and saw three men standing near him. When he saw them, he ran from the tent entrance to meet them, and bowed down to the ground. He said, "My lord, if I find favor with you, do not pass by your servant. Let a little water be brought, and wash your feet, and rest yourselves under the tree. Let me bring a little bread, that you may refresh yourselves, and after that you may pass on—since you have come to your servant." So they said, "Do as you have said." And Abraham hastened into the tent to Sarah, and said, "Make ready quickly three measures of choice flour, knead it, and make cakes." Abraham ran to the herd, and took a calf, tender and good, and gave it to the servant, who hastened to prepare it. Then he took curds and milk and the calf that he had prepared, and set it before them; and he stood by them under the tree while they ate.

The word of the Lord.

Leader:	Friends, this reading tells a wonderful story about hospitality. Abraham was the very embodiment of welcome. Three strangers suddenly appear out of nowhere and Abraham treats them as if they were close relatives or friends, washing their feet, having a feast prepared, and standing by them as they ate, anticipating their needs. This story should inspire us to offer this same kind of welcome to each and every person who enters our church. We may not have a freshly slaughtered calf to offer people. What we do have to offer them is a greater feast—nourishment at the table of God's word as well as the very body and blood of the Lord Jesus. Just as Abraham did, we, too, must extend hospitality to those we see week after week, as well as strangers who visit us. In this way, people will be drawn to listen to the holy word of God, and be welcomed at the table of the Eucharist.

Response
Romans 12:9–13

Leader:	**May we welcome Christ in one another.**
All:	May we welcome Christ in one another.
Leader:	**Let love be genuine; hate what is evil, hold fast to what is good.**
All:	May we welcome Christ in one another.
Leader:	**Love one another with mutual affection; outdo one another in showing honor.**
All:	May we welcome Christ in one another.
Leader:	**Do not lag in zeal, be ardent in spirit, serve the Lord.**
All:	May we welcome Christ in one another.
Leader:	**Rejoice in hope, be patient in suffering, persevere in prayer.**
All:	May we welcome Christ in one another.
Leader:	**Contribute to the needs of the saints; extend hospitality to strangers.**
All:	May we welcome Christ in one another.

The leader invites all to rise.

Leader: Friends, inspired by the example of the Lord Jesus, who welcomed tax collectors and sinners, and ate with them, let us pray now in the words he gave us. Our Father . . .

CLOSING PRAYER

Leader: Let us pray.
God of Abraham and Sarah,
we look to you to be our strength
as we seek to become more zealous ministers of hospitality.
Inspire us to break out of any behavior that prevents us
from extending a warm welcome to all who enter our church.
Renew us in our dedication to care for friend and stranger alike,
for in welcoming them, we welcome you.
We ask this through Christ our Lord.

All: Amen.

BLESSING AND DISMISSAL

Leader: Let our response be "Amen" to each blessing prayer.

May God bless us in our ministry of hospitality and continue to reveal the presence of Christ in one another. R/. Amen.

May the Holy Spirit inspire us to share the very presence of God with all who enter our church. R/. Amen.

May the Lord Jesus continue to renew us as we strive to follow the way of hospitality, which he extended so generously to all who sought healing and reconciliation. R/. Amen.

Leader: Peace is a sure sign of welcome and hospitality. To conclude our prayer service, let us offer one another a sign of Christ's peace.

The prayer service may conclude with an appropriate song.

PRAYER SERVICES FOR PARISH LIFE © 2004, World Library Publications • 800-566-6150 • WLP 017264. Scripture quotations are from the New Revised Standard Version of the Bible © 1989 by the Division of Christian Education of the National Council of the Churches of Christ in the USA. All rights reserved. Used with permission.

PRAYER SERVICE FOR MINISTERS OF CARE

A vessel of oil should be placed on a table in a prominent area of the prayer space. The Lectionary may be placed on the table as well, surrounded by flowers and candles.

The leader invites all to rise.

The prayer service may begin with an appropriate song.

Leader: Let us begin by signing ourselves with the sign of our faith. In the name of the Father, ✠ and of the Son, and of the Holy Spirit.

All: Amen.

Leader: Friends, as ministers of care, we are called to bring the healing presence of Christ to those who are ill and confined. It is good for us to take time to refresh ourselves and be renewed in our ministry of care. Let this prayer service remind us of the importance of our ministry and strengthen us in our commitment to serve those who are most in need.

OPENING PRAYER

Leader: Let us pray.
God of everlasting goodness,
you sent your Son among us
to bring healing, peace, and reconciliation to our weary world.
As we continue his ministry of care,
renew us in mind, body, and spirit.
May Christ's healing presence flow through us
as we serve those entrusted to our care.
We ask this in his name,
Christ the healer,
who is Lord forever and ever.

All: Amen.

The leader invites all to be seated.

READING OF THE WORD OF GOD

First Reading
James 5:13–16

Are any among you suffering? They should pray. Are any cheerful? They should sing songs of praise. Are any among you sick? They should call for the elders of the church and have them pray over them, anointing them with oil in the name of the Lord. The prayer of faith will save the sick, and the Lord will raise them up.

The word of the Lord.

Response
Psalm 63

Leader: O God, you are my God, I seek you,
      my soul thirsts for you;
  my flesh faints for you,
      as in a dry and weary land where there is no water.

All: So I have looked upon you in the sanctuary,
      beholding your power and glory.
  Because your steadfast love is better than life,
      my lips will praise you.
  So I will bless you as long as I live;
      I will lift up my hands and call on your name.

Leader: My soul is satisfied as with a rich feast,
      and my mouth praises you with joyful lips
  when I think of you on my bed,
      and meditate on you in the watches of the night.

All: For you have been my help,
      and in the shadow of your wings I sing for joy.
  My soul clings to you;
      your right hand upholds me.

Gospel *(All rise.)*
Matthew 11:28–30

Jesus said, "Come to me, all you that are weary and are carrying heavy burdens, and I will give you rest. Take my yoke upon you, and learn from me; for I am gentle and humble in heart, and you will find rest for your souls. For my yoke is easy, and my burden is light."
The Gospel of the Lord.

RITUAL ANOINTING

The leader stands at the table upon which is placed the vessel of oil.

The leader invites all to rise.

Leader: Brothers and sisters, the Church uses oil to anoint the sick. Since ancient times oil has been a symbol of strength for the one being anointed. We now ask God to strengthen us in our ministry as our hands are anointed. May this anointing renew us in our ministry of care.

Let us pray.
God of everlasting love,
we come to you seeking your gentleness and compassion.
Help us to find rest for our souls
even in the midst of life's burdens.
Strengthen us with this anointing.
May our hands be the hands of Christ,
bringing hope to those who have fallen into despair.
Keep us always close to you
and lead us one day into your heavenly kingdom.
We ask this through Christ our Lord.

All: Amen.

The leader invites the ministers of care to come forward. As each person's hands are anointed with the oil, the leader says, "May your hands be the hands of Christ."

Once the anointing has been concluded, the leader may wish to wash his or her hands. Moist towelettes work best!

Leader: Sisters and brothers, let us now pray in the words our Savior gave us. Our Father . . .

BLESSING AND DISMISSAL

Leader: Let our response be "Amen" to each blessing prayer.

May God strengthen us in our ministry to bring the care of the Church to all in need. R/. Amen.

Leader: May Christ dwell in our hearts and fill us with gentleness and compassion. R/. Amen.

Leader: May the Holy Spirit continue to renew us in mind, body, and spirit as we rededicate ourselves to the ministry of care. R/. Amen.

Leader: As a sign of our oneness in this ministry, and to conclude our service, let us extend to one another a sign of Christ's peace.

The prayer service may conclude with an appropriate song.

PRAYER SERVICE FOR EXTRAORDINARY MINISTERS OF COMMUNION

Before the prayer service, a large fresh loaf of bread (not sliced) should be placed in a dish and set on a table in the center of the prayer space. The assembly should be seated in a circle, facing the center.

The leader invites all to rise.

The prayer service may begin with an appropriate song.

Leader: Let us begin by signing ourselves with the sign of our faith. In the name of the Father, ✠ and of the Son, and of the Holy Spirit. Brothers and sisters, we are entrusted with an extraordinary ministry. We come together to pray that we will be renewed in mind and heart as we endeavor to grow closer to the Lord, who is made present in the Eucharist. Let us take this opportunity to ask God to instill in us a longing to grow closer to the Lord Jesus.

OPENING PRAYER

Leader: Let us pray.

God of abundant life,
you call us to serve your people
as extraordinary ministers of Communion.
Take hold of us this night (day)
and lead us into greater union
with your Son.
Open our hearts to your sacred word,
which feeds us and sustains us.
We ask this through Christ our Lord.

All: Amen.

The leader invites all to be seated.

Reading of the Word of God

First Reading
Acts 2:42–47

The disciples devoted themselves to the apostles' teaching and fellowship, to the breaking of bread and the prayers.

Awe came upon everyone, because many wonders and signs were being done by the apostles. All who believed were together and had all things in common; they would sell their possessions and goods and distribute the proceeds to all, as any had need. Day by day, as they spent much time together in the temple, they broke bread at home and ate their food with glad and generous hearts, praising God and having the goodwill of all the people. And day by day the Lord added to their number those who were being saved.

The word of the Lord.

Response
Psalm 78:3–4, 23–24, 25, 54

Leader:	**Things that we have heard and known,**
	        that our ancestors have told us,
	            we will tell to the coming generations
	    the glorious deeds of the LORD, and his might
	        and the wonders that he has done.

All:	Yet he commanded the skies above,
	        and opened the doors of heaven;
	    he rained down on them manna to eat,
	        and gave them the grain of heaven.

Leader:	**Mortals ate of the bread of angels;** **he sent them food in abundance.**
All:	He brought them to his holy hill, to the mountain that his right hand had won.

Gospel *(All rise.)*
Luke 24:13–35

Now on that same day two of them were going to a village called Emmaus, about seven miles from Jerusalem, and talking with each other about all these things that had happened. While they were talking and discussing, Jesus himself came near and went with them, but their eyes were kept from recognizing him. And he said to them, "What are you discussing with each other while you walk along?" They stood still, looking sad. Then one of them, whose name was Cleopas, answered him, "Are you the only stranger in Jerusalem who does not know the things that have taken place there in these days?" He asked them, "What things?" They replied, "The things about Jesus of Nazareth, who was a prophet mighty in deed and word before God and all the people, and how our chief priests and leaders handed him over to be condemned to death and crucified him. But we had hoped that he was the one to redeem Israel. Yes, and besides all this, it is now the third day since these things took place. Moreover, some women of our group astounded us. They were at the tomb early this morning, and when they did not find his body there, they came back and told us that they had indeed seen a vision of angels who said that he was alive. Some of those who were with us went to the tomb and found it just as the women had said; but they did not see him." Then he said to them, "Oh, how foolish you are, and how slow of heart to believe all that the prophets have declared! Was it not necessary that the Messiah should suffer these things and then enter into his glory?" Then beginning with Moses and all the prophets, he interpreted to them the things about himself in all the scriptures.

As they came near the village to which they were going, he walked ahead as if he were going on. But they urged him strongly, saying, "Stay with us, because it is almost evening and the day is now nearly over." So he went in to stay with them. When he was at the table with them, he took bread, blessed and broke it, and gave it to them. Then their eyes were opened, and they recognized him; and he vanished from their sight. They said to each other, "Were not our hearts burning within us while he was talking to us on the road, while he was opening the scriptures to us?" That same hour they got up and returned to Jerusalem; and they found the eleven and their companions gathered together. They were saying, "The Lord has risen indeed, and he has appeared to Simon!" Then they told what had happened on the road, and how he been made known to them in the breaking of the bread.

The Gospel of the Lord.

Leader: Brothers and sisters, this remarkable story has much to tell us about our own ministry. Each time we gather for Mass, the Lord Jesus is made present to us in the breaking of the bread. Each of us has been deeply moved as we have shared the Eucharist with our parish family. I am now going to ask you to recall a moment when you experienced the Lord Jesus in this ministry—a moment when you came to know the Lord Jesus more deeply.

REFLECTIVE SILENCE

The leader then takes the loaf of bread and shares a personal story of how Jesus became known to him or her during the ministry of sharing the body and blood of Christ with others. At the conclusion of the sharing, the leader breaks off a small piece of the bread and consumes it.

Leader: We will now pass this loaf around the room. I would ask that you tell your own story of how you have experienced the Lord in this ministry. At the conclusion of your story, break off a piece of the bread, consume it, then pass the loaf to the person next to you.

If there is a large number of ministers present, several loaves may be used and the people may gather in smaller groups.

At the conclusion of the sharing, the leader asks the ministers to rise.

Leader: Friends, the two disciples on the road to Emmaus recognized Jesus in the breaking of the bread. We have just experienced the presence of Jesus as we have shared our stories and broken this bread. Now let us ask God to strengthen us in our ministry.

Let our response be: "Our hearts are burning within us."

When we hear your word, O Lord: R/.

When we lift up our voices in song, O Lord: R/.

When we gather with our community of faith, O Lord: R/.

When we receive your body and blood, O Lord: R/.

When we share that body and blood with your people, O Lord: R/.

When we contemplate your presence in the Eucharist, O Lord: R/.

Let us now ask God to give us our daily bread by reciting together the Lord's Prayer. Our Father . . .

BLESSING AND DISMISSAL

Leader: Brothers and sisters, let us respond "Amen" to each blessing prayer.
May God bless us in our ministry and strengthen us in faith. R/. Amen.

Leader: May the Lord Jesus find a dwelling place within our hearts. R/. Amen.

Leader: May the Holy Spirit draw us into the holy communion of the Blessed Trinity. R/. Amen.

Leader: Friends, as a sign of mutual support in this ministry, let us conclude this prayer by extending to one another a sign of Christ's peace.

The prayer service may conclude with an appropriate song.

PRAYER SERVICE FOR MUSIC MINISTERS

The leader invites all to rise.

The prayer service may begin with an appropriate song.

Leader: Let us begin by signing ourselves with the sign of our faith. In the name of the Father, ✠ and of the Son, and of the Holy Spirit.

Brothers and sisters, we stand in awe in the presence of our God, who has generously poured out the gift of music on our community through the talents of each one gathered here. Whether we play an instrument, sing, or conduct, we each contribute to making a joyful sound unto the Lord week after week in our parish. As members of the Body of Christ, we often give that Body ways to express its joy, its pain, its grief, and its wonder. For this we are forever grateful to God.

OPENING PRAYER

Leader: Let us pray.
God of abundant life,
you have called us to serve your people
as ministers of music.
Your Son, Jesus Christ,
is your everlasting song of goodness, truth, and peace.
Baptized into his image, we continue his song of hope
for a world often lost in darkness and despair.
Open our hearts to welcome your sacred word,
which feeds us and sustains us.
We ask this through Christ our Lord.

All: Amen.

The leader invites all to be seated.

READING OF THE WORD OF GOD

First Reading
2 Chronicles 5:11–14

The priests came out of the holy place (for all the priests who were present had sanctified themselves, without regard to their divisions, and all the levitical singers, Asaph, Heman, and Jeduthun, their sons and kindred, arrayed in fine linen, with cymbals, harps, and lyres, stood east of the altar with one hundred twenty priests who were trumpeters.) It was the duty of the trumpeters and singers to make themselves heard in unison in praise and thanksgiving to the Lord, and when the song was raised, with trumpets and cymbals and other musical instruments, in praise to the Lord,

"For he is good,
for his steadfast love endures forever,"

the house, the house of the LORD, was filled with a cloud, so that the priests could not stand to minister because of the cloud; for the glory of the LORD filled the house of God.

The word of the Lord.

or

Colossians 3:12–17

As God's chosen ones, holy and beloved, clothe yourselves with compassion, kindness, humility, meekness, and patience. Bear with one another and, if anyone has a complaint against another, forgive each other; just as the Lord has forgiven you, so you also must forgive. Above all, clothe yourselves with love, which binds everything together in perfect harmony. And let the peace of Christ rule in your hearts, to which indeed you were called in the one body. And be thankful. Let the word of Christ dwell in you richly; teach and admonish one another in all wisdom; and with gratitude in your hearts sing psalms, hymns, and spiritual songs to God. And whatever you do, in word or deed, do everything in the name of the Lord Jesus, giving thanks to God the Father through him.

The word of the Lord.

Response
Psalm 81:1–2, Isaiah 42:10–11, Psalm 92:1–4, Psalm 98:1–6

Leader:	**Sing aloud to God our strength;** **shout for joy to the God of Jacob.**
All:	Raise a song, sound the tambourine, the sweet lyre with the harp. Blow the trumpet at the new moon, at the full moon on our festal day.
Leader:	**Sing to the LORD a new song,** **his praise from the end of the earth!** **Let the sea roar and all that fills it,** **the coastlands and their inhabitants.**

All: Let the desert and its towns lift up their voice,
the villages that Kedar inhabits;
let the inhabitants of Sela sing for joy,
let them shout from the tops of the mountains.

**Leader: It is good to give thanks to the LORD,
to sing praises to your name, O Most High.**

All: To declare your steadfast love in the morning,
and your faithfulness by night,
to the music of the lute and the harp,
to the melody of the lyre.
For you, O LORD, have made me glad by your work;
at the works of your hands I sing for joy.

**Leader: O sing to the LORD a new song,
for he has done marvelous things.
His right hand and his holy arm
have gotten him victory.**

All: The LORD has made known his victory;
he has revealed his vindication in the sight of the nations.
He has remembered his steadfast love and faithfulness
to the house of Israel.
All the ends of the earth have seen
the victory of our God.

**Leader: Make a joyful noise to the LORD, all the earth;
break forth into joyous song and sing praises.**

All: Sing praises to the LORD with the lyre,
with the lyre and the sound of melody.
With trumpets and the sound of the horn
make a joyful noise before the King, the LORD.

Gospel *(All rise.)*
Matthew 26:26–30

While they were eating, Jesus took a loaf of bread, and after blessing it he broke it, gave it to the disciples, and said, "Take, eat; this is my body." Then he took a cup, and after giving thanks he gave it to them, saying, "Drink from it, all of you; for this is my blood of the covenant, which is poured out for many for the forgiveness of sins. I tell you, I will never again drink of this fruit of the vine until that day when I drink it new with you in my Father's kingdom."

When they had sung the hymn, they went out to the Mount of Olives.

The Gospel of the Lord.

INTERCESSIONS

Leader: **Sisters and brothers, God calls us to use our talents to help build the kingdom of God here on earth. As musicians, we help bring that kingdom to a reality by creating rhythms and sounds that give God's people a taste of the life to come. Let us praise God.**

O God, you are the giver of every good gift.

All: Thank you for the gifts you have so generously given us.

Leader: **O God, you created the music of nature that fills the earth.**

All: Help us be attuned to the music of creation that surrounds us.

Leader: **O God, you filled your people, Israel, with a song of praise and thanksgiving.**

All: May their song uphold us in our ministry.

Leader: **O God, you gave voice to the psalmist.**

All: May the singing of psalms continue to inspire us.

Leader: **O God, you sent your Son to be your song of mercy and salvation.**

All: May his song be on our lips and in our hearts.

Leader: **O God, you continue to create music by sending us gifted artists and composers.**

All: Bless their work and lead them closer to your heart.

Leader: **O God, you bless us with voices to sing; with mouths, hands, and feet to play instruments; with ears to hear and to refine our skills.**

All: Bless us, O God, as we make a joyful sound to your name.

Leader: Let us lift our voices in song and pray in the words that the Lord Jesus gave us. Our Father . . .

CLOSING PRAYER

Leader: Let us pray.
O God of wonder,
you have created us in your own image and likeness.
In you is the very beauty of music itself.
Keep our hearts faithful to the call
we received in baptism:
to bring a song of hope to those who despair;
a song of comfort to the sorrowing;
a song of elation to the joyful;
and a song of healing to the sick.
We ask this in the name of your Son and our song,
our Lord Jesus Christ,
who lives and reigns with you and the Holy Spirit.
You are one God forever and ever.

All: Amen.

Leader: Friends, to conclude this celebration, let us offer one another a sign of Christ's peace.

The prayer service may conclude with an appropriate song.

PRAYER SERVICES FOR PARISH LIFE © 2004, World Library Publications • 800-566-6150 • WLP 017264. Bible Text: New Revised Standard Version Bible © 1989, Division of Christian Education of the National Council of the Churches of Christ in the United States of America. All rights reserved. Used with permission.

PRAYER SERVICE FOR ALTAR SERVERS

Leader: We gather together to thank God for the opportunities we have to become closer to Jesus Christ as we serve at Mass. Let us listen to God's word.

READING OF THE WORD OF GOD

Acts 2:42–47

The disciples devoted themselves to the apostles' teaching and fellowship, to the breaking of bread and the prayers.

Awe came upon everyone, because many wonders and signs were being done by the apostles. All who believed were together and had all things in common; they would sell their possessions and goods and distribute the proceeds to all, as any had need. Day by day, as they spent time together in the temple, they broke bread at home and ate their food with glad and generous hearts, praising God and having the goodwill of all the people. And day by day the Lord added to their number those who were being saved.

The word of the Lord.

Leader: Friends, in this reading from the Acts of the Apostles, we are told that the early followers of Jesus prayed and worked together so that no one would be in need. You serve at the altar of God so that the people of our parish will be able to celebrate well together. When we are fed with Christ's body and blood, we then can go forth to bring God's good news to the poor and everyone in need. Your work inspires people, young and old alike, to have a special love for the Eucharist. Let us now ask God to strengthen all of us as we strive to be altar servers who not only perform our ministry well, but do so with love for God and each other.

The leader invites all to rise.

Leader: O God, you call us to serve at your altar.

All: Give us the help we need to be dedicated servers.

Leader: O God, you gave us your only Son to be our redeemer.

All: Strengthen us to be more and more like Christ.

Leader: O God, you gave us the gift of the Eucharist as a living reminder of your love for us.

All: Help us to show awe and reverence for the Eucharist.

Leader:	O God, you are always with us.
All:	Be with us when we are in need.
Leader:	Let us now pray in the words that Jesus himself gave us. Our Father . . .

CLOSING PRAYER

Leader:	Let us pray. O God of love, thank you for the opportunity to serve you as we serve the people of this parish. Help us to be focused on our ministry. May the holy work we do in church be reflected in our everyday lives. We ask this through Christ our Lord.
All:	Amen.
Leader:	Let us now ask for God's blessing. Please respond "Amen" after each blessing prayer. May God, who created all things for us, bless us. R/. Amen.
Leader:	May Jesus Christ, who is our salvation, keep us in God's love. R/. Amen.
Leader:	May the Holy Spirit, who is our help, strengthen us in our ministry. R/. Amen.
Leader:	To conclude this prayer service, let us share a sign of peace with one another.

PRAYER SERVICES FOR PARISH LIFE © 2004, World Library Publications • 800-566-6150 • WLP 017264. Bible Text: New Revised Standard Version Bible © 1989, Division of Christian Education of the National Council of the Churches of Christ in the United States of America. All rights reserved. Used with permission.

Prayer Service for a Meeting of the Liturgy Committee

Before the service, the Lectionary for Mass and the Roman Missal are placed on a table in the center of the prayer space. Flowers and candles may be placed there as well.

The leader invites all to rise.

The prayer service may begin with an appropriate song.

Leader: As in all things, we are gathered by our God, who is Father, ✠ Son, and Holy Spirit.

Friends, each time we come together as a committee we are focused on preparing the sacred liturgy for our community. Let us now spend time renewing ourselves at the table of God's word. Let us ask God to strengthen us in our ministry.

Opening Prayer

Leader: Let us pray.
O God of everlasting goodness,
be with us at this hour of promise.
You have called us to prepare the worship of this community.
Renew in us a sense of awe in your presence,
manifested in the sacramental life of our parish.
Just as your Son gathered his disciples in the upper room,
so may we be gathered to give praise and honor to your name.
We ask this through Christ our Lord.

All: Amen.

The leader invites all to be seated.

READING OF THE WORD OF GOD

First Reading
Ephesians 4:1–7, 11–13

Brothers and sisters, I, therefore, the prisoner in the Lord, beg you to lead a life worthy of the calling to which you have been called, with all humility and gentleness, with patience, bearing with one another in love, making every effort to maintain the unity of the Spirit in the bond of peace. There is one body and one Spirit, just as you were called to the one hope of your calling, one Lord, one faith, one baptism, one God and Father of all, who is above all and through all and in all.

But each of us was given grace according to the measure of Christ's gift.

The gifts he gave were that some would be apostles, some prophets, some evangelists, some pastors and teachers, to equip the saints for the work of ministry, for building up the body of Christ, until all of us come to the unity of the faith and of the knowledge of the Son of God, to maturity, to the measure of the full stature of Christ.

The word of the Lord.

Response
Psalm 100:1–5

Leader:	**Make a joyful noise to the LORD, all the earth.**
All:	Worship the LORD with gladness; come into his presence with singing.
Leader:	**Know that the LORD is God.**
All:	It is he that made us, and we are his; we are his people, and the sheep of his pasture.
Leader:	**Enter his gates with thanksgiving, and his courts with praise.**
All:	Give thanks to him, bless his name.
Leader:	**For the LORD is good;**
All:	His steadfast love endures forever, and his faithfulness to all generations.

Gospel *(All rise.)*
Matthew 26:17–19

On the first day of Unleavened Bread the disciples came to Jesus, saying, "Where do you want us to make the preparations for you to eat the Passover?" He said, "Go into the city to a certain man, and say to him, 'The Teacher says, My time is near; I will keep the Passover at your house with my disciples.' " So the disciples did as Jesus had directed them, and they prepared the Passover meal.

The Gospel of the Lord.

RECOMMITMENT TO MINISTRY

Leader: Dear friends, the Church's two major liturgical books, the Lectionary for Mass and the Roman Missal, are placed before us. These are our primary tools for preparing the worship for our parish. These books contain the sacred word of God, as well as the prayers that embody the traditions of the Church. In these texts we are given God's inspired words, as well as words that direct our ritual gesture. As people entrusted with the care of the liturgy, we help to bring life to these words, which, in turn, can bring life to our people. As we know, this is no easy task. Each of us brings different gifts to this important work.

Just as the disciples were instructed to prepare the Passover supper for the Lord Jesus, so, too, are we instructed to prepare the liturgy for our parish. As a sign of our commitment to this ministry, and to witness faithfully to the saving words contained in these books, each of us now approaches the table, in silence. When standing before the table, place one hand on the Lectionary and the other on the Roman Missal. Pray that you will be a worthy instrument of God. Pray that the people of our parish will grow closer to the Lord through our efforts. And, finally, pray that your own relationship with the Lord Jesus will be renewed.

Each committee member approaches the table, lays hands on the books, and prays in silence.

INTERCESSIONS

Leader: Friends, God's holy word, as well as the sacred words and actions of the Church, inspire us to grow closer in our relationship with Jesus Christ. Let us pray now that we will be renewed in that relationship.

Reader: That we will continue to be inspired by the celebration of the Church's rites, we pray to the Lord.

Reader: That the words and actions of the liturgy will move us to work for justice for those who are in need, we pray to the Lord.

Reader: That our efforts to prepare the Church's rites will lead to deeper participation in the liturgy by all the members of our community, we pray to the Lord.

Reader: That we will all be led to that full, conscious, and active participation in the liturgy called for by the Church, we pray to the Lord.

Reader: That we will be renewed in our ministry as we prepare the liturgy with care, respect, and a deep sense of the active presence of the Holy Spirit, we pray to the Lord.

Leader: Let us gather all our prayers into one and raise our hands to heaven, praying in the words our Savior gave us. Our Father . . .

BLESSING AND DISMISSAL

Leader: Brothers and sisters, let us respond "Amen" to each blessing prayer.

May God our creator bless us in our ministry and strengthen us in faith. R/. Amen.

Leader: May the Lord Jesus find a dwelling place within our hearts. R/. Amen.

Leader: May the Holy Spirit inspire us in our work and deepen our sense of awe before the Lord, made manifest in the Church's liturgy. R/. Amen.

Leader: Friends, as a sign of mutual support in this ministry, let us conclude this prayer by extending to one another a sign of Christ's peace.

The prayer service may conclude with an appropriate song.

PRAYER SERVICES FOR PARISH LIFE © 2004, World Library Publications • 800-566-6150 • WLP 017264. Bible Text: New Revised Standard Version Bible © 1989, Division of Christian Education of the National Council of the Churches of Christ in the United States of America. All rights reserved. Used with permission.

PRAYER SERVICE FOR VOLUNTEER APPRECIATION

The paschal candle should be placed in a prominent location and lighted before the service begins. Each participant should be a given a candle (like those used at the Easter Vigil).

The leader invites all to rise.

The prayer service may begin with an appropriate song.

Leader: Brothers and sisters, we gather to give praise and thanks to God for the gifts so generously bestowed on our parish through your commitment to work to further God's reign. The Lord is lavish in giving gifts that can be placed at the service of the people of God. You have chosen to respond to God's call. For this, the people of this parish are most grateful.

OPENING PRAYER

Leader: Let us pray.

God of peace,
in baptism you call us to be Christ for one another.
Having responded to that call,
we come before you in thanksgiving
for all the good works you have accomplished through us.
Continue to nourish us through word and sacrament
and may our efforts lead your people closer
to the reign of promised peace.
We make our prayer through Christ our Lord.

All: Amen.

The leader invites all to be seated.

READING OF THE WORD OF GOD

First Reading
Philippians 4:4–9

Brothers and sisters, Rejoice in the Lord always; again I will say, Rejoice. Let your gentleness be known to everyone. The Lord is near. Do not worry about anything, but in everything by prayer and supplication with thanksgiving let your requests be made known to God. And the peace of God, which surpasses all understanding, will guard your hearts and minds in Christ Jesus.

Finally, beloved, whatever is true, whatever is honorable, whatever is just, whatever is pure, whatever is pleasing, whatever is commendable, if there is any excellence and if there is anything worthy of praise, think about these things. Keep on doing the things that you have learned and received and heard and seen in me, and the God of peace will be with you.

The word of the Lord.

Response
Psalm 112:1–9

Leader: **Praise the Lord!**
Happy are those who fear the LORD,
who greatly delight in his commandments.
Their descendants will be mighty in the land;
the generation of the upright will be blessed.

All: Wealth and riches are in their houses,
and their righteousness endures forever.
They rise in the darkness as a light for the upright;
they are gracious, merciful, and righteous.

Leader: **It is well with those who deal generously and lend,**
who conduct their affairs with justice.
For the righteous will never be moved;
they will be remembered forever.

All: They are not afraid of evil tidings;
their hearts are firm, secure in the LORD.
Their hearts are steady; they will not be afraid;
in the end they will look in triumph on their foes.
They have distributed freely, they have given to the poor;
their righteousness endures forever.

Gospel *(All rise.)*
Matthew 5:13–16

Jesus said, "You are the salt of the earth; but if salt has lost its taste, how can its saltiness be restored? It is no longer good for anything, but is thrown out and trampled under foot.

"You are the light of the world. A city built on a hill cannot be hid. No one after lighting a lamp puts it under the bushel basket, but on the lampstand, and it gives light to all in the house. In the same way, let your light shine before others, so that they may see your good works and give glory to your Father in heaven."

The Gospel of the Lord.

RECOMMITMENT TO PARISH MINISTRY AND SERVICE

Leader: Brothers and sisters, on the day of baptism, we were each given a candle and told to keep the flame bravely burning. The Lord Jesus tells us that we are the salt of the earth and the light of the world. Each of us casts out the darkness by letting our light shine in service of God's people. We now light our candles as a reminder of our baptism. We are also reminded that we are called to continue to spread the light to all we meet.

Several people come forward, light their candles, and spread the light to others.

Leader: Sisters and brothers, are you willing to share the light of Christ with others?

All: We are.

Leader: Do you promise never to hide your light, but always keep it burning in service to God's people?

All: We do.

Leader: Are you willing to respond with love to those who seek the living God?

All: We are.

Leader: Friends, we praise and thank God for the great gifts planted in each one of us at the moment of our baptism. We ask God to continue to nurture us on our journeys of faith and to help us keep the flame of faith bravely burning. In thanksgiving to God, let us all join in praying Psalm 138.

Psalm 138:1a, 2–5

All: I give you thanks, O LORD, with my whole heart.
I bow down toward your holy temple
  and give thanks to your name for your steadfast love
   and your faithfulness;
  for you have exalted your name and your word
  above everything.

On the day I called you answered me,
  you increased my strength of soul.

All the kings of the earth shall praise you, O LORD,
  for they have heard the words of your mouth.
They shall sing the ways of the LORD,
  for great is the glory of the LORD.

If certificates of appreciation are to be awarded, all extinguish their candles and the certificates are presented.

CLOSING PRAYER

Leader: **Gracious God,
our hearts are filled with gratitude
for your mercy and compassion.
You give us every good gift
and ask us to place those gifts at the service of your people.
Thank you for your generosity
in instilling within each of us
a commitment to serve your people.
Strengthen us on our own journeys of faith
and lead us one day to the enjoyment of everlasting peace,
which you promised through your Son, our Lord Jesus Christ.
We make our prayer in his name,
who is Lord forever and ever.**

All: Amen.

Leader: **May God bless us, ✠
protect us from all evil,
and bring us to everlasting life.**

All: May God strengthen us in faith,
keep us in hope,
and shower us with love. Amen.

The prayer service may conclude with an appropriate song.

PRAYER SERVICE TO WELCOME NEW PARISHIONERS

This short prayer service can be celebrated in conjunction with a parish information session or social event welcoming new parishioners.

The leader invites all to rise.

Leader: Our parish is blessed and enriched by the presence of new parishioners *(if possible name the new parishioners)*. Our prayer is that they will find in this place a home where they can bring their sorrows and joys, their pain and triumphs.

OPENING PRAYER

Leader: Let us pray.
O God of love and mercy,
you walked with your people, Israel, through the wilderness
and brought them to the promised land.
We ask you to continue to walk with your people,
especially those who have found a parish home here among us.
May they know your presence
as it is revealed in our celebration of the sacraments,
in your holy word,
in those who lead us,
and in the faces of those who gather here each week for worship.
We ask this in the name of your Son, Jesus Christ,
who is Lord forever and ever.

All: Amen.

The leader invites all to be seated.

READING OF THE WORD OF GOD
Romans 12:3–5, 12–13

Brothers and sisters: For by the grace given to me I say to everyone among you not to think of yourself more highly than you ought to think, but to think with sober judgment, each according to the measure of faith that God has assigned. For as in one body we have many members, and not all the members have the same function, so we, who are many, are one body in Christ, and individually we are members one of another.

Rejoice in hope, be patient in suffering, persevere in prayer. Contribute to the needs of the saints; extend hospitality to strangers.

The word of the Lord.

Response
Psalm 100:1–5

All: Make a joyful noise to the LORD, all the earth.

Worship the LORD with gladness;
     come into his presence with singing.

Know that the LORD is God.
     It is he that made us, and we are his;
     we are his people, and the sheep of his pasture.

Enter his gates with thanksgiving,
     and his courts with praise.
     Give thanks to him, bless his name.

For the LORD is good;
     his steadfast love endures forever,
     and his faithfulness to all generations.

The leader invites all to rise.

Leader: **Uniting our voices, let us now pray in the words our Savior gave us. Our Father . . .**

CLOSING PRAYER

Leader: **Let us pray.**
God of the covenant,
we rejoice in your presence
made visible among us through our new parish members.
May they be welcomed in this community
and find here a family of love and support.
Through our celebration of the liturgy,
our catechetical, social, and justice ministries,
may we work together to continue your reign
inaugurated by the work of your Son,
who is Lord forever and ever.

All: Amen.

Leader: **Let us conclude this prayer service by offering each other a sign of Christ's peace.**

PRAYER SERVICES FOR PARISH LIFE © 2004, World Library Publications • 800-566-6150 • WLP 017264. Scripture quotations are from the New Revised Standard Version of the Bible © 1989 by the Division of Christian Education of the National Council of the Churches of Christ in the USA. All rights reserved. Used with permission.

Prayer for a Parish Meeting

At the Beginning of the Meeting

Leader: **Let us pray for God's help
and the inspiration of the Holy Spirit during our meeting.**

Reading of the Word of God
2 Corinthians 4:13–15

**But just as we have the same spirit of faith that is in accordance with scripture—
"I believed, and so I spoke" — we also believe, and so we speak, because we know
that the one who raised the Lord Jesus will raise us also with Jesus, and will bring
us with you into his presence. Yes, everything is for your sake, so that grace, as it
extends to more and more people, may increase thanksgiving, to the glory of God.
The word of the Lord.**

Response
Job 33:3–4

All: My words declare the uprightness of my heart
     and what my lips know they speak sincerely.
The spirit of God has made me,
     and the breath of the Almighty gives me life.

Intercessions

Leader: **We are gathered in the Spirit.
Let us open our minds and hearts to the needs of our parish.
Let our response be "Lord, hear our prayer."**

Reader: That we may put aside any self-interest
in favor of the good of the entire parish community,
we pray to the Lord. R/.

That each member of this
council/committee/commission/society/association/body
may openly express ideas, problems, and projects
for mature consideration by everyone present,
we pray to the Lord. R/.

That our parish community may always respond
to the needs of all its members
regardless of age or social status,
we pray to the Lord. R/.

We may pause to add our own intentions, aloud or in silence.

Leader:	**O God, you have heard our prayer for your assistance.**
	We believe we are gathered here in your Spirit.
	Strengthen our faith, hope, and love,
	and bring our efforts to a fruitful resolution.
	We ask this through Christ our Lord.
All:	Amen.

AT THE CLOSE OF THE MEETING

READING OF THE WORD OF GOD
Ephesians 3:14–19

For this reason I bow my knees before the Father, from whom every family in heaven and on earth takes its name. I pray that, according to the riches of his glory, he may grant that you may be strengthened in your inner being with power through his Spirit, and that Christ may dwell in your hearts through faith, as you are being rooted and grounded in love. I pray that you may have the power to comprehend, with all the saints, what is the breadth and length and height and depth, and to know the love of Christ that surpasses knowledge, so that you may be filled with all the fullness of God.

The word of the Lord.

Response
Ephesians 3:20–21

All:	Now to him who by the power at work within us
	is able to accomplish abundantly far more
	than all we can ask or imagine,
	to him be glory in the church and in Christ Jesus to all generations
	forever and ever. Amen.

PRAYER SERVICES FOR PARISH LIFE © 2004, World Library Publications • 800-566-6150 • WLP 017264. Scripture quotations are from the New Revised Standard Version of the Bible © 1989 by the Division of Christian Education of the National Council of the Churches of Christ in the USA. All rights reserved. Used with permission.

PARISH PICNIC

The prayer service may begin with an appropriate song.

CALL TO CELEBRATION

Leader: **God looked at everything that had been made.**

All: And found it very good.

OPENING PRAYER

Leader: **Let us pray.**
Lord our God,
we celebrate this opportunity to be together,
cheered by the love of one another
and surrounded by the natural beauty of the earth.
Let the things of earth refresh us
and increase our awareness of the beauty
in one another and in you.
We ask this through Christ our Lord.

All: Amen.

READING OF THE WORD OF GOD
Matthew 6:26–33

Jesus said, "Look at the birds of the air; they neither sow nor reap nor gather into barns, and yet your heavenly Father feeds them. Are you not of more value than they? And can any of you by worrying add a single hour to your span of life? And why do you worry about clothing? Consider the lilies of the field, how they grow; they neither toil nor spin, yet I tell you, even Solomon in all his glory was not clothed like one of these. But if God so clothes the grass of the field, which is alive today and tomorrow is thrown into the oven, will he not much more clothe you—you of little faith? Therefore do not worry, saying, 'What will we eat?' or 'What will we drink?' or 'What will we wear?' For it is the Gentiles who strive for these things, and indeed your heavenly Father knows that you need all these things. But strive first for the kingdom of God and his righteousness and all these things will be given to you as well."

The word of the Lord.

BLESSING OF FOOD

Leader: Our help comes from the LORD.

All:

Who made heaven and earth.   *Psalm 121:2*

Leader: Let us pray.

O God, by your word all things are made holy.
Bless this food
[hamburgers, hot dogs, marshmallows, salads, cookies, watermelon . . .]
that you have created.
Grant that whoever gives thanks to you
and uses it in accordance with your law and your will
may receive health of body and protection of soul
by calling on your holy name.
We ask this through Christ our Lord.

All: Amen.

CONCLUDING RITE

At the close of the picnic, all gather in thanksgiving.

Leader: Please respond "We thank you, Lord" after each invocation.

For this time to enjoy the earth,
one another, and you, O Lord:
R/. We thank you, Lord.

For the beautiful sight of sunshine and flowers,
grass and trees, butterflies, and gliding birds: R/.

For the delightful sounds of calling birds,
rushing water, and crackling campfires: R/.

For the enjoyable scents of fresh air,
roasting hot dogs, and steaming coffee: R/.

For the pleasant touch of grass and sand,
the warmth of the sun,
the stimulation of the wind and water: R/.

For this time to re-create ourselves
in body, mind, and spirit: R/.

For the refreshment of exercise,
the calm away from the pressures of work: R/.

For this relaxed time to renew the bonds of love
sometimes overlooked in the routine of daily work: R/.

For all who try to make this earth a better place to live: R/.

DEPARTURE

Leader: **Let us return home refreshed in body and spirit.**

All: Thanks be to God.

The prayer service may conclude with an appropriate song.

Prayer before a Parish Trip

The prayer service may begin with an appropriate song.

CALL TO WORSHIP

Leader: **May we be blessed in the city,
and blessed in the country!**

All: May we be blessed in our coming in,
and blessed in our going out!

OPENING PRAYER

Leader: **Let us pray.**

**Lord, hear our prayers
and graciously accompany us in our travel.
Grant us a happy journey and a peaceful time
that we may safely reach our destination,
return in joy to our home,
and come finally to the haven of eternal salvation.
We ask this through Christ our Lord.**

All: Amen.

READING OF THE WORD OF GOD
Joshua 24:17, 18b

It is the LORD our God who brought us and our ancestors up from the land of Egypt, out of the house of slavery, and who did those great signs in our sight. He protected us along all the way that we went, and among all the peoples through whom we passed. Therefore we also will serve the LORD, for he is our God.

The word of the Lord.

Response
Psalm 121:5, 8

All: The LORD is our keeper;
the LORD is our shade at our right hand.
The LORD will keep our going out and our coming in
from this time on and forevermore.

PRAYER

Leader: **O God, you have given your angels charge over us,**

All: To guard us in all our undertakings.

Leader: **Let us pray.**
O God, we marvel at your providence,
which has given your holy angels care over us.
You protected your people, Israel,
on their sojourn in the desert.
Watch over us in our travels.
Listen to our prayers for your blessing,
that we may be safe under your protection
and happy in your company through all eternity.
We ask this through Christ our Lord.

All: Amen.

CONCLUDING RITE

Leader: **May the almighty and merciful Lord**
lead us along ways of peace and contentment,
and may the angel Raphael accompany us on our journey,

All: So we may return to our home
in peace, health, and joy.

The prayer service may conclude with an appropriate song.

PRAYER SERVICES FOR PARISH LIFE © 2004, World Library Publications • 800-566-6150 • WLP 017264. Scripture quotations are from the New Revised Standard Version of the Bible © 1989 by the Division of Christian Education of the National Council of the Churches of Christ in the USA. All rights reserved. Used with permission.

CELEBRATING THE GIFT OF GOD'S CREATION

We celebrate our blessings and pray that all people may protect these gifts from needless, selfish destruction. This service may be celebrated outdoors in a place of natural beauty.

The prayer service may begin with an appropriate song.

CALL TO CELEBRATION

Leader: **Open your eyes, your hearts, your whole selves, and sense the good things we have from the Lord our God.**

All: Blessed be our God forever.

OPENING PRAYER

Leader: **Let us pray.**

Creator of the universe, we are your people.
You bless our earth with natural beauty and wealth.
Show us the way to use these blessings without destroying them.
Increase our appreciation for clean air, pure water,
and the breathtaking beauty of the natural landscape.
May our lifetime here enable others to have
such blessings in future generations.

We ask this in your holy name, God forever and ever.

All: Amen.

READING OF THE WORD OF GOD.
Deuteronomy 8:7–14

For the LORD your God is bringing you into a good land, a land with flowing streams, with springs and underground waters welling up in valleys and hills, a land of wheat and barley, of vines and fig trees and pomegranates, a land of olive trees and honey, a land where you may eat bread without scarcity, where you will lack nothing, a land whose stones are iron and from whose hills you may mine copper. You shall eat your fill and bless the LORD your God for the good land that he has given you.

Take care that you do not forget the LORD your God, by failing to keep his commandments, his ordinances, and his statutes, which I am commanding you today. When you have eaten your fill and have built fine houses and live in them, and when your herds and flocks have multiplied, and your silver and gold is multiplied, and all that you have is multiplied, then do not exalt yourself, forgetting the LORD your God.

The word of the Lord.

LITANY OF PRAISE AND THANKSGIVING
(In the style of Daniel 3:52–90)

Leader: **Blest are you, O Lord, the God of creation.**
All: Praiseworthy and exalted forever.

Leader: **Blest are you, Lord of the nations.**
All: Praiseworthy and exalted forever.

Leader: **Bless the Lord, all you works of the Lord.**
All: Praise and exalt God forever.

Leader: **Northern lights and sunny days, bless the Lord.**
All: Praise and exalt God forever.

Leader: **Twinkling stars and darkest night, bless the Lord.**
All: Praise and exalt God forever.

Leader: **Sky and clouds and heaven above, bless the Lord.**
All: Praise and exalt God forever.

Leader: **Dew and fog and glistening frost, bless the Lord.**
All: Praise and exalt God forever.

Leader: **All you winds, bless the Lord.**
All: Praise and exalt God forever.

Leader: **All you seasons, bless the Lord.**
All: Praise and exalt God forever.

Leader: **Tundra and deserts, fields and plains, bless the Lord.**
All: Praise and exalt God forever.

Leader: **All mountains and hills, bless the Lord.**
All: Praise and exalt God forever.

Leader: **All lakes and ponds, bless the Lord.**
All: Praise and exalt God forever.

Leader: **All rivers and streams, bless the Lord.**
All: Praise and exalt God forever.

Leader: **Hot springs, geysers, and fountains, bless the Lord.**
All: Praise and exalt God forever.

Leader: **Coal mines, gold and silver mines, gravel pits, and oil wells, bless the Lord.**
All: Praise and exalt God forever.

Leader: **All you animals wild and tame, bless the Lord.**
All: Praise and exalt God forever.

| Leader: | All you birds of the air, bless the Lord. |
| All: | Praise and exalt God forever. |

| Leader: | All you fish in the shallows and depths, bless the Lord. |
| All: | Praise and exalt God forever. |

| Leader: | All you natural resources and wealth of this land, bless the Lord. |
| All: | Praise and exalt God forever. |

| Leader: | All you commerce and industry, business and trade, bless the Lord. |
| All: | Praise and exalt God forever. |

| Leader: | Church bells, school bells, and cow bells, bless the Lord. |
| All: | Praise and exalt God forever. |

| Leader: | Cities and towns, suburbs, farms, and ranches, bless the Lord. |
| All: | Praise and exalt God forever. |

| Leader: | Automobiles and trains, airplanes and ships, bless the Lord. |
| All: | Praise and exalt God forever. |

| Leader: | Bicycles, scooters, wagons, and all moving things, bless the Lord. |
| All: | Praise and exalt God forever. |

| Leader: | Train whistles, factory whistles, and all whistles, bless the Lord. |
| All: | Praise and exalt God forever. |

| Leader: | Skyscrapers and hotels, hogans and teepees, bungalows and apartments, bless the Lord. |
| All: | Praise and exalt God forever. |

| Leader: | Citizens of this land, bless the Lord. |
| All: | Praise and exalt God forever. |

A talk or discussion may follow this litany. Participants could prepare slides or other presentations. These activities may initiate and stimulate local ecological programs.

CONCLUDING RITE

| Leader: | Filled with God's praises, we return home glorifying the Lord. May peace be with us all, now and forever. |
| All: | Amen. |

The prayer service may conclude with an appropriate song.

ADVENT PENITENTIAL SERVICE

The leader invites all to rise.

The prayer service may begin with an appropriate song.

CALL TO WORSHIP
Isaiah 55:6

Leader: **Seek the LORD while he may be found,**
call upon him while he is near.

All: Let us turn our hearts to the LORD,
whose mercy knows no end.

Leader: **Lord Jesus, you were foretold by the prophets:**
Lord, have mercy.

All: Lord, have mercy.

Leader: **Lord Jesus, you came to save us from sin:**
Christ, have mercy.

All: Christ, have mercy.

Leader: **Lord Jesus, you are the Light who scatters the darkness of sin:**
Lord, have mercy.

All: Lord, have mercy.

OPENING PRAYER

Leader: **Let us pray.**
God of all ages,
your only Son became flesh
to free us from the bondage of sin.
Help us now to cleanse our souls
and to prepare room in our hearts,
that we may be ready to meet him when he comes.
We ask this through Christ our Lord.

All: Amen.

The leader invites all to seated.

READING OF THE WORD OF GOD

First Reading
1 John 1:5 — 2:2

This is the message we have heard from him and proclaim to you, that God is light and in him there is no darkness at all. If we say that we have fellowship with him while we are walking in darkness, we lie and do not do what is true; but if we walk in the light as he himself is in the light, we have fellowship with one another, and the blood of Jesus his Son cleanses us from all sin. If we say that we have no sin, we deceive ourselves, and the truth is not in us. If we confess our sins, he who is faithful and just will forgive us our sins and cleanse us from all unrighteousness. If we say that we have not sinned, we make him a liar, and his word is not in us.

My little children, I am writing these things to you so that you may not sin. But if anyone does sin, we have an advocate with the Father, Jesus Christ the righteous; and he is the atoning sacrifice for our sins, and not for ours only but also for the sins of the whole world.

The word of the Lord.

Response
Psalm 25:8–11

All: Good and upright is the LORD;
      therefore he instructs sinners in the way.
     He leads the humble in what is right,
      and teaches the humble his way.
     All the paths of the LORD are steadfast love and faithfulness,
      for those who keep his covenant and his decrees.
     For your name's sake, O LORD,
      pardon my guilt, for it is great.

Gospel *(All rise.)*
John 3:16–21

"For God so loved the world that he gave his only Son, so that everyone who believes in him may not perish but may have eternal life.

"Indeed, God did not send the Son into the world to condemn the world, but in order that the world might be saved through him. Those who believe in him are not condemned; but those who do not believe are condemned already, because they have not believed in the name of the only Son of God. And this is the judgment, that the light has come into the world, and people loved darkness rather than light because their deeds were evil. For all who do evil hate the light and do not come to the light, so that their deeds may not be exposed. But those who do what is true come to the light, so that it may be clearly seen that their deeds have been done in God."

The Gospel of the Lord.

EXAMINATION OF CONSCIENCE
(See pages 72–74 for examples)

The leader invites all to kneel or bow and join in a formula for confession, such as:

All: I confess to Almighty God,
and to you, my brothers and sisters,
that I have sinned through my own fault
(All strike their breast.)
in my thoughts and in my words,
in what I have done,
and in what I have failed to do;
and I ask blessed Mary, ever virgin,
all the angels and saints,
and you, my brothers and sisters,
to pray for me to the Lord our God.

All then stand and pray Psalm 51.

Psalm 51:1–17

Leader: **Have mercy on me, O God,**
      according to your steadfast love;
according to your abundant mercy
      blot out my transgressions.
Wash me thoroughly from my iniquity,
      and cleanse me from my sin.

All: For I know my transgressions,
      and my sin is ever before me.
Against you, you alone, have I sinned,
      and done what is evil in your sight,
so that you are justified in your sentence
      and blameless when you pass judgment.

Leader: **Indeed, I was born guilty,**
      a sinner when my mother conceived me.
You desire truth in the inward being;
      therefore teach me wisdom in my secret heart.

All: Purge me with hyssop, and I shall be clean;
      wash me, and I shall be whiter than snow.
Let me hear joy and gladness;
      let the bones that you have crushed rejoice.
Hide your face from my sins,
      and blot out all my iniquities.

Leader: Create in me a clean heart, O God,
and put a new and right spirit within me.
Do not cast me away from your presence,
and do not take your holy spirit from me.
Restore to me the joy of your salvation,
and sustain in me a willing spirit.

All: Then I will teach transgressors your ways,
and sinners will return to you.
Deliver me from bloodshed, O God,
O God of my salvation,
and my tongue will sing aloud of your deliverance.

Leader: O Lord, open my lips,
and my mouth will declare your praise.
For you have no delight in sacrifice;
if I were to give a burnt offering, you would not be pleased.

All: The sacrifice acceptable to God is a broken spirit;
a broken and contrite heart, O God, you will not despise.

Leader: Let us now pray that we will be forgiven our sins as we forgive the sins of others. Our Father . . .

Leader: Holy God,
we stand ready to accept the Prince of Peace
into our hearts.
As Christmas draws near,
draw us ever closer to him whose coming we await.
He is Lord forever and ever.

All: Amen.

[INDIVIDUAL CONFESSION AND ABSOLUTION]

PROCLAMATION OF PRAISE FOR GOD'S MERCY
Luke 1:46–55

All: My soul magnifies the Lord,
    and my spirit rejoices in God my Savior,
for he has looked with favor on the lowliness of his servant.
    Surely, from now on all generations will call me blessed;
for the Mighty One has done great things for me,
    and holy is his name.
His mercy is for those who fear him
    from generation to generation.
He has shown strength with his arm;
    he has scattered the proud in the thoughts of their hearts.
He has brought down the powerful from their thrones,
    and lifted up the lowly;
he has filled the hungry with good things,
    and sent the rich away empty.
He has helped his servant Israel,
    in remembrance of his mercy,
according to the promise he made to our ancestors,
    to Abraham and to his descendants forever.

CLOSING PRAYER

Leader: **Gracious God,**
your people have cried out to you for mercy.
Listen to our prayer of thanksgiving
for your outpouring of forgiveness.
Lead us away from deeds of darkness
until we know the light that never fades.
As we await the coming of the Light of the World,
heal us, renew us,
and keep us ever close to you.
We ask this through Christ our Lord.

All: Amen.

DISMISSAL

Leader: **Go in peace,**
and may Jesus the Light shine on your path
and in your heart forever.

All: Thanks be to God.

The prayer service may conclude with an appropriate song.

LENTEN PENITENTIAL SERVICE

The leader invites all to rise.

The prayer service may begin with an appropriate song.

CALL TO WORSHIP
Lamentations 3:40–41

Leader: **Let us test and examine our ways,
                and return to the LORD.**

All: Let us lift up our hearts as well as our hands
                to God in heaven.

OPENING PRAYER

Leader: **Let us pray.**

           Merciful Lord,
           we ask forgiveness of our sins.
           As we hear your scriptures
           help us to heed your invitation to repent.
           May we know ourselves in need of your mercy.
           Help us to make Lent a preparation
           for the glory that is to come.
           We ask this through Christ our Lord.

All: Amen.

The leader invites all to be seated.

READING OF THE WORD OF GOD

First Reading
Hosea 14:1–3, 9

Return, O Israel, to the LORD your God,
>   for you have stumbled because of your iniquity.

Take words with you
>   and return to the LORD;

say to him,
>   "Take away all guilt;

accept that which is good,
>   and we will offer
>   the fruit of our lips.

Assyria shall not save us;
>   we will not ride upon horses;

we will say no more, 'Our God,'
>   to the work of our hands.

In you the orphan finds mercy."
For the ways of the Lord are right,
>   and the upright walk in them,
>   but transgressors stumble in them.

The word of the Lord.

Response
Psalm 119:89, 28, 105

Leader: The LORD exists forever;
>   your word is firmly fixed in heaven.

All: My soul melts away for sorrow;
>   strengthen me according to your word.

Leader: Your word is a lamp to my feet
>   and a light to my path.

Gospel *(All rise.)*
John 20:19–23

When it was evening on that day, the first day of the week, and the doors of the house where the disciples had met were locked for fear of the Jews, Jesus came and stood among them and said, "Peace be with you." After he said this, he showed them his hands and his side. Then the disciples rejoiced when they saw the Lord. Jesus said to them again, "Peace be with you. As the Father has sent me, so I send you." When he had said this, he breathed on them and said to them, "Receive the Holy Spirit. If you forgive the sins of any, they are forgiven them; if you retain the sins of any, they are retained."

The Gospel of the Lord.

Examination of Conscience
(See pages 72–74 for examples)

The leader invites all to kneel or bow and join in a formula for confession, such as:

All: I confess to Almighty God,
and to you, my brothers and sisters,
that I have sinned through my own fault
(All strike their breast.)
in my thoughts and in my words,
in what I have done,
and in what I have failed to do;
and I ask blessed Mary, ever virgin,
all the angels and saints,
and you, my brothers and sisters,
to pray for me to the Lord our God.

The leader then invites all to rise.

Litany

Leader: **At an acceptable time I have listened to you,
and on a day of salvation I have helped you.**   *2 Corinthians 6:2*

All: The kindness of God leads us to repentance.

Leader: **Come now, let us argue it out,
says the LORD:
though your sins are like scarlet,
they shall be like snow;
though they are red like crimson,
they shall become like wool.**   *Isaiah 1:18*

All: Cleanse me from my sin.
Wash me, and I shall be whiter than snow.   *Psalm 51:2, 7b*

Leader: **Come, let us walk in the light of the Lord!**

All: The night is far gone, the day is near.
Let us then lay aside the works of darkness
and put on the armor of light.   *Romans 13:12*

Resolution

Leader: **Our God acts not out of whimsy but by careful design. Thus all the important acts of salvation have followed a period of purification and preparation.**

All: For everything there is a season,
and a time for every matter under heaven.   *Ecclesiastes 3:1*

Leader:	**Before the covenant with the human race was made with Noah, a period of rain separated the just from the unjust.**
All:	The rain fell on the earth forty days and forty nights. *Genesis 7:12*
Leader:	**Before the covenant was given on Mount Sinai, Moses underwent a period of preparation.**
All:	Moses entered the cloud, and went up on the mountain. Moses was on the mountain for forty days and forty nights. *Exodus 24:18*
Leader:	**Before the prophet Elijah could commune with God, he had to undergo a period of pilgrimage.**
All:	Elijah got up, and ate and drank; then he went in the strength of that food forty days and forty nights to Horeb the mount of God. *1 Kings 19:8*
Leader:	**Before the beginning of his public ministry, Jesus experienced a period of testing in the desert.**
All:	Jesus, full of the Holy Spirit, returned from the Jordan and was led by the Spirit in the wilderness, where for forty days he was tempted by the devil. *Luke 4:1–2*
Leader:	**Before his return to the Father, the risen Lord prepared the disciples for the church's mission.**
All:	After his suffering he presented himself alive to them by many convincing proofs, appearing to them during forty days and speaking about the kingdom of God. *Acts 1:3*
Leader:	**Now we are gathered to celebrate another period of forty days, a period of preparation whose goal is the glory of Easter.**
All:	Therefore, since we are surrounded by so great a cloud of witnesses, let us also lay aside every weight and the sin that clings so closely, and let us run with perseverance the race that is set before us, looking to Jesus the pioneer and perfecter of our faith, who for the sake of the joy that was set before him endured the cross, disregarding its shame, and has taken his seat at the right hand of the throne of God. *Hebrews 12:1–2*
Leader:	**Let us now pray that we will be forgiven our sins as we forgive the sins of others. Our Father . . .**

Leader: Holy God,
          now is the acceptable time to return to you.
          As we walk the path of these forty days,
          may we turn away from sin
          and embrace a life of goodness and truth.
          Strengthen us on our Lenten journey
          and keep us focused on the cross and resurrection
          of your Son, our Savior and redeemer.
          He is Lord forever and ever.

All: Amen.

[INDIVIDUAL CONFESSION AND ABSOLUTION]

PROCLAMATION OF PRAISE FOR GOD'S MERCY
Ephesians 1:3–8a

All: Blessed be the God and Father of our Lord Jesus Christ,
          who has blessed us in Christ with every spiritual blessing
          in the heavenly places,
          just as he chose us in Christ
          before the foundation of the world
          to be holy and blameless before him in love.
          He destined us for adoption as his children
          through Jesus Christ,
          according to the good pleasure of his will,
          to the praise of his glorious grace
          that he freely bestowed on us in the Beloved.
          In him we have redemption through his blood,
          the forgiveness of our trespasses,
          according to the riches of his grace
          that he lavished on us.

CLOSING PRAYER

Leader: Gracious God,
          for forty days and nights
          your Son was tempted by the devil in the desert.
          We have entered the Lenten desert of repentance.
          Purify and enlighten us
          so that we may inherit the rewards of everlasting life.
          We make our prayer through Christ our Lord.

All: Amen.

DISMISSAL

Leader: **Having been renewed in heart and mind,
go in the peace of Christ.**

All: Thanks be to God.

The prayer service may conclude with an appropriate song.

Penitential Service: Hope

The leader invites all to rise.

The prayer service may begin with an appropriate song.

CALL TO WORSHIP
Psalm 62:7–8

Leader: **On God rests my deliverance and my honor;
my mighty rock, my refuge is in God.**

All: Trust in him at all times, O people;
pour out your hearts before him;
God is a refuge for us.

OPENING PRAYER

Leader: **Let us pray.**

**Merciful God,
your Son's cross has freed us.
In our frailty we have misused the gift of freedom.
We seek deliverance from the slavery of sin.
Help us to grow in the love of your commandments,
that in obedience to your will we may find perfect freedom.
We ask this through Christ our Lord.**

All: Amen.

The leader invites all to be seated.

READING OF THE WORD OF GOD

First Reading
Job 11:13–18

**"If you direct your heart rightly
you will stretch out your hands toward him.
If iniquity is in your hand, put it far away,
and do not let wickedness reside in your tents.
Surely then you will lift up your face without blemish;
you will be secure and will not fear.
You will forget your misery;
you will remember it as waters that have passed away.
And your life will be brighter than the noonday;
its darkness will be like the morning.
And you will have confidence, because there is hope;
you will be protected and take your rest in safety."
The word of the Lord.**

Gospel *(All rise.)*
John 14:1–3, 18–19

Jesus said, "Do not let your hearts be troubled. Believe in God, believe also in me. In my Father's house there are many dwelling places. If it were not so, would I have told you that I go to prepare a place for you? And if I go and prepare a place for you, I will come again and will take you to myself, so that where I am, there you may be also.

"I will not leave you orphaned; I am coming to you. In a little while the world will no longer see me, but you will see me; because I live, you also will live."

The Gospel of the Lord.

EXAMINATION OF CONSCIENCE
(See pages 72–74 for examples)

The leader invites all to kneel or bow and join in a formula for confession, such as:

All:　　　I confess to Almighty God,
　　　　　and to you, my brothers and sisters,
　　　　　that I have sinned through my own fault
　　　　　(All strike their breast.)
　　　　　in my thoughts and in my words,
　　　　　in what I have done,
　　　　　and in what I have failed to do;
　　　　　and I ask blessed Mary, ever virgin,
　　　　　all the angels and saints,
　　　　　and you, my brothers and sisters,
　　　　　to pray for me to the Lord our God.

The leader then invites all to rise.

LITANY

Leader:　　**Let us rejoice in hope;**
　　　　　let us be patient under trial;
　　　　　let us persevere in prayer.

Reader:　　As we strive to admonish the sinner,
　　　　　and as we are aware of our sins:

All:　　　**R/.** We trust in your help, O Lord.

Reader:	As we attempt to instruct the ignorant,
	and as we admit our own ignorance of the ways of God:
	R/.
	As we try to counsel the doubtful,
	and as we attempt to live with our doubts:
	R/.
	As we seek to comfort the sorrowful,
	and as we succumb to self-pity:
	R/.
	As we strive to bear wrongs patiently,
	and as we find it hard to forgive all injuries:
	R/.
	As we are mindful of the living and the dead,
	and as we pray for their eternal happiness:
	R/.

Leader: **Let us now pray that we will be forgiven our sins as we forgive the sins of others. Our Father . . .**

Leader: **God our Creator,**
you cleanse us in the regeneration of baptism
and purify us in the sacrament of reconciliation.
Strengthen our profession of trust in your Son,
whose promises deserve our trust.
Help us to rouse one another to generosity and service,
that we may encourage all
by our example of faith, hope, and love.
We ask this through Christ our Lord.

All: Amen.

[INDIVIDUAL CONFESSION AND ABSOLUTION]

PROCLAMATION OF PRAISE FOR GOD'S MERCY
Acts 2:25–28

All: I saw the Lord always before me,
for he is at my right hand so that I will not be shaken;
therefore my heart was glad, and my tongue rejoiced;
moreover my flesh will live in hope.
For you will not abandon my soul to Hades,
or let your Holy One experience corruption.
You have made known to me the ways of life;
you will make me full of gladness with your presence.

CLOSING PRAYER

Leader: Gracious God,
we rejoice in the hope of the promises made by your Son, Jesus.
Turn our hearts away from sin and
help us to embrace a life of mercy and compassion.
We ask this in the name of Christ the Lord.

All: Amen.

DISMISSAL

Leader: Living in joyful hope for the coming of the Lord,
we go forth in the peace of Christ.

All: Thanks be to God.

The prayer service may conclude with an appropriate song.

PENITENTIAL SERVICE: A NEW BEGINNING

With special New Year rites, ancient peoples endeavored to abolish the past so that there could be a new birth of times. After rites of purification, confession of sin, and exorcism, the people entered another cycle of time. They were refreshed and reborn in spirit. In our time, New Year's resolutions reflect these efforts to make things new. This is a new year. Before much of it slips into the past, we take time to consider this new beginning.

The leader invites all to rise.

The prayer service may begin with an appropriate song.

CALL TO A NEW BEGINNING
Ephesians 5:8–9

Leader: **Once we were darkness.**

All: Now in the Lord we are light.

Leader: **The fruit of the light is found in all that is good and right and true.**

All: Let us live as children of the light.

OPENING PRAYER

Leader: **Let us pray.**
Almighty Father,
when time began you were the Lord of that moment.
As this new year advances, you are Lord of each moment.
May you who stand at the beginning of time and beyond it
guide us in our use of time during this year.
We ask this through Christ our Lord.

All: Amen.

The leader invites all to be seated.

READING OF THE WORD OF GOD

First Reading
Hosea 6:1–3
"Come, let us return to the LORD;
for it is he who has torn, and he will heal us;
he has struck down, and he will bind us up.
After two days he will revive us;
on the third day he will raise us up,
that we may live before him.
Let us know, let us press on to know the LORD;
his appearing is as sure as the dawn;
he will come to us like the showers,
like the spring rains that water the earth."
The word of the Lord.

RESPONSE

Leader:	**Creative love of the Father,**
All:	Renew the face of the earth.
Leader:	**Jesus among us,**
All:	Renew the face of the earth.
Leader:	**Continuing guidance of the Holy Spirit,**
All:	Renew the face of the earth.
Leader:	**Caring for one another,**
All:	We are people of light.
Leader:	**With sacrifices throughout the year,**
All:	We are people of light.
Leader:	**Giving food to the hungry and drink to the thirsty,**
All:	We are people of light.
Leader:	**Clothing the naked and sheltering the homeless,**
All:	We are people of light.
Leader:	**Visiting the imprisoned and the sick,**
All:	We are people of light.
Leader:	**Burying the dead,**
All:	We are people of light.
Leader:	**Shedding our selfishness and sin,**
All:	We are people of light.
Leader:	**Forgiving one another,**
All:	We are people of light.

Gospel *(All rise.)*
Luke 13:6–9

Then he told this parable: "A man had a fig tree planted in his vineyard; and he came looking for fruit on it and found none. So he said to the gardener, 'See here! For three years I have come looking for fruit on this fig tree, and still I find none. Cut it down! Why should it be wasting the soil?' He replied, 'Sir, let it alone for one more year, until I dig around it and put manure on it. If it bears fruit next year, well and good; but if not, you can cut it down.' "
The Gospel of the Lord.

Pause for reflection after each thought. The leader may also offer a brief reflection based on these ideas.

The signs of life I give to others are . . .

My tree of life bears fruit when . . .

Jesus' light shines through me when . . .

For the New Year I will try . . .

Examination of Conscience
(See pages 72–74 for examples)

The leader invites all to kneel or bow and join in a formula for confession, such as:

All: I confess to Almighty God,
and to you, my brothers and sisters,
that I have sinned through my own fault
(*All strike their breast.*)
in my thoughts and in my words,
in what I have done,
and in what I have failed to do;
and I ask blessed Mary, ever virgin,
all the angels and saints,
and you, my brothers and sisters,
to pray for me to the Lord our God.

The leader then invites all to rise.

Leader: **God our Father,
we worship you as our first beginning,
our constant help and protection,
and the source of our everlasting happiness.
With your wisdom, guide us through this New Year.
May we courageously accept all its duties
and advance through all it holds for us.
Help us to rise above our human weaknesses,
that we may forgive the wrongs against us
as you forgive us our offenses.
Let us forget ourselves
and reach out to others in peace and love.
Father, may we be one with you forever,
through Jesus, the Lord.**

All: Amen.

Leader: **Let us now pray that we will be forgiven our sins as we forgive the sins of others. Our Father . . .**

[Individual Confession and Absolution]

PROCLAMATION OF PRAISE FOR GOD'S MERCY
Isaiah 12:1–2, 4b–6

All: I will give thanks to you, O LORD,
    for though you were angry with me,
  your anger turned away,
    and you comforted me.

  Surely God is my salvation;
    I will trust, and will not be afraid,
  for the LORD GOD is my strength and my might;
    he has become my salvation.

  Give thanks to the LORD,
    call on his name;
  make known his deeds among the nations;
    proclaim that his name is exalted.

  Sing praise to the LORD, for he has done gloriously;
    let this be known in all the earth.
  Shout aloud and sing for joy, O royal Zion,
    for great in your midst is the Holy One of Israel.

CLOSING PRAYER

Leader: **Let us pray.**

**Almighty Father, a new year has dawned over the earth,
and we pray for your gift of peace.
Grant that the joy that fills our hearts during this season
may bring harmony to our homes and places of work.
Let your Son's light shine on our world's uncertainties.
May all of us come to live with you forever.**

We ask this through Christ our Lord.

All: Amen.

DISMISSAL

Leader: **May the almighty Lord order our days and deeds in peace,
and lead us to everlasting light.**

All: Amen.

The prayer service may conclude with an appropriate song.

Penitential Service: Respect for Life

The leader invites all to rise.

The prayer service may begin with an appropriate song.

Call to Worship

Leader: **Blessed be the God and Father of our Lord Jesus Christ!
By his great mercy he has given us a new birth into a living hope
through the resurrection of Jesus Christ
from the dead.**

1 Peter 1:3

All: In him we live and move and have our being.

Acts 17:28

Opening Prayer

Leader: **Let us pray.**

**O God, our eyes behold the beauty of your creation,
and our ears catch the sounds of your power.
We hold our lives sacred because they are your gift.
Bring us to greater awareness of the sanctity of human life
and to sorrow for the times we have ignored or offended it.
We ask this through Christ our Lord.**

All: Amen.

The leader invites all to be seated.

Reading of the Word of God

First Reading
Deuteronomy 30:15–20a

See, I have set before you today life and prosperity, death and adversity. If you obey the commandments of the LORD your God that I am commanding you today, by loving the LORD your God, walking in his ways, and observing his commandments, decrees, and ordinances, then you shall live and become numerous, and the LORD your God will bless you in the land that you are entering to possess. But if your heart turns away and you do not hear, but are led astray to bow down to other gods and serve them, I declare to you today that you shall perish; you shall not live long in the land that you are crossing the Jordan to enter and possess. I call heaven and earth to witness against you today that I have set before you life and death, blessings and curses. Choose life so that you and your descendants may live, loving the LORD your God.

The word of the Lord.

Response
Psalm 27:1, 13

All: The LORD is my light and my salvation;
    whom shall I fear?
The LORD is the stronghold of my life,
    of whom shall I be afraid?
I believe that I shall see the goodness of the LORD
    in the land of the living.

Gospel *(All rise.)*
Matthew 25:31–40

Jesus said, "When the Son of Man comes in his glory, and all the angels with him, then he will sit on the throne of his glory. All the nations will be gathered before him, and he will separate people one from another as a shepherd separates the sheep from the goats, and he will put the sheep at his right hand and the goats at the left. Then the king will say to those at his right hand, 'Come, you that are blessed by my Father, inherit the kingdom prepared for you from the foundation of the world; for I was hungry and you gave me food, I was thirsty and you gave me something to drink, I was a stranger and you welcomed me, I was naked and you gave me clothing, I was sick and you took care of me, I was in prison and you visited me.' Then the righteous will answer him, 'Lord, when was it that we saw you hungry and gave you food, or thirsty and gave you something to drink? And when was it that we saw you a stranger and welcomed you, or naked and gave you clothing? And when was it that we saw you sick or in prison and visited you?' And the king will answer them, 'Truly I tell you, just as you did it to one of the least of these who are members of my family, you did it to me.' "

The Gospel of the Lord.

INTERCESSIONS

Leader: **All life comes from God.**
With lively faith we ask God's blessing on the living.

Reader: For a greater realization of the sanctity of marriage,
that parents may be conscious of their calling
as they share in God's creative power, we pray to the Lord.

For governments and all civil legislators,
that they may enact laws
that uphold God's fundamental law
and every person's right to life, we pray to the Lord.

For those who have acted against human life,
that they may know the wrong
and experience forgiveness, we pray to the Lord.

For those whose lives are threatened by illness or accident,
for those responsible for preserving the sacredness of life,
and for ourselves, that we may show greater concern for all,
we pray to the Lord.

For young people everywhere,
that they may respect life and love,
we pray to the Lord.

EXAMINATION OF CONSCIENCE
(See pages 72–74 for examples)

The leader invites all to kneel or bow and join in a formula for confession, such as:

All: I confess to Almighty God,
and to you, my brothers and sisters,
that I have sinned through my own fault
(All strike their breast.)
in my thoughts and in my words,
in what I have done,
and in what I have failed to do;
and I ask blessed Mary, ever virgin,
all the angels and saints,
and you, my brothers and sisters,
to pray for me to the Lord our God.

The leader then invites all to rise.

Leader: **Let us now pray that we will be forgiven our sins as we forgive the
sins of others. Our Father . . .**

[INDIVIDUAL CONFESSION AND ABSOLUTION]

CLOSING PRAYER

Leader: God our Father,
you showed us how much we mean to you
when you sent Jesus, your Son, into our world.
He died for us to demonstrate your love.
We pray that we may imitate the lessons of his life
and today's lessons in all life's encounters.
May our respect for one another increase.
When we improve the quality of life,
let it be for all, not just those whom we know.
We ask this through Christ our Lord.

All: Amen.

BLESSING

Leader: Let our response be "Amen" to each blessing prayer.

May God the Creator bless and guide us
in the way of righteousness. R/. Amen.

May God the Redeemer teach us respect for the sanctity of life
and lead us to eternal life. R/. Amen.

May God the Sanctifier strengthen our wills to uphold faithfully
each person's human dignity. R/. Amen.

A priest or deacon adds:
May almighty God bless you,
the Father, and the Son, and the Holy Spirit. R/. Amen.

The prayer service may conclude with an appropriate song.

PRAYER SERVICES FOR PARISH LIFE © 2004, World Library Publications • 800-566-6150 • WLP 017264. Scripture quotations are from the New Revised Standard Version of the Bible © 1989 by the Division of Christian Education of the National Council of the Churches of Christ in the USA. The English translation of the *Confiteor* from *The Roman Missal* © 1973, International Committee on English in the Liturgy, Inc. All rights reserved. Used with permission.

Examination of Conscience Based on the Beatitudes

Matthew 5:3–11

Blessed are the poor in spirit, for theirs is the kingdom of heaven.

What are my priorities?

Do I focus too much on the things of this earth?

Do I share my gifts, talents, time, and treasure to help build the kingdom of God here on earth?

Blessed are those who mourn, for they will be comforted.

Do I take the time for prayer, calling out to God in my need?

Do I, in turn, try to assist those who are suffering?

Blessed are the meek, for they will inherit the earth.

Do I ever look down on others because they may not look or act like me?

Do I treat other people fairly—at work, at school, at home?

Do I think that I have all the answers?

Are my close relationships nurtured by mutual respect?

Blessed are those who hunger and thirst for righteousness, for they will be filled.

When I see or hear stories of people suffering injustice, what is my response?

Do the places where I allocate my money reflect a thirst for justice?

Blessed are the merciful, for they will receive mercy.

When I am wronged, am I willing to forgive?

Am I currently holding any grudges against anyone?

Blessed are the pure in heart, for they will see God.

Do I respect the gift of my body, created in God's image?

When I hear a dirty or racist joke, do I turn away?

Blessed are the peacemakers, for they will be called children of God.

Do I work for peace in my community, neighborhood, and family?

Blessed are those who are persecuted for righteousness' sake, for theirs is the kingdom of heaven.

If a conversation about religion begins in the workplace or a social event, am I willing to add my own concerns, based on my Catholic faith, to that conversation?

Am I willing to take a stand that is unpopular, but is based on gospel values?

Blessed are you when people revile you and persecute you and utter all kinds of evil against you falsely on my account. Rejoice and be glad, for your reward is great in heaven.

Am I willing to forgive others when they speak about me harshly?

Is my life on this earth focused on the life to come?

EXAMINATION OF CONSCIENCE IN LITANY FORM

The leader should pause after each statement, allowing the participants time for reflection.

O God, you have created us in your image and likeness, called to be people faithful to you—in worship, prayer, and action.

O God, in baptism you made us your children, called to be a people faithful to your commands.

O God, you sent the Holy Spirit, the giver of life, to cultivate in us a deep reverence for all human life.

O God, you sent your Son, Jesus Christ, who called us to give water to the thirsty, food to the hungry, and shelter to the homeless.

O God, you call us to faithful worship in the name of your Son, Jesus Christ.

O God, you call us to respect the property of others.

O God, you call us to treasure the gift of our own human bodies.

O God, you call us to reach out in loving service to all.

EXAMINATION OF CONSCIENCE BASED ON MATTHEW 25: 31–46

In the twenty-fifth chapter of the Gospel of Saint Matthew, we hear the familiar story of the separation of the sheep from the goats at the end of time. The Lord Jesus grants eternal life to those who, by the way they lived their lives, extended charity and justice to those in need. For those who ignored the needs of others, eternal punishment was their inheritance. Let us ponder these words as we ask God for mercy. Let us also pray for a change of heart.

"I was hungry and you gave me food. I was thirsty and you gave me something to drink."

Have I shared out of my own gifts to help others?

Have I given in to our society's seemingly endless appetite for possessions?

"I was a stranger and you welcomed me."

What is my attitude toward those who may be of a different race, religious expression, or social status?

Am I a person who practices Christian hospitality?

When I encounter a stranger, do I offer a warm welcome?

"I was naked and you gave me clothing."

What is my attitude toward the poor?

Have I taken a real inventory of the clothes I own, in order to share with those who are in need?

Am I overly concerned with the way I am dressed, while others struggle with the little clothing they have to keep them warm and safe from the elements?

"I was sick and you took care of me."

When a friend or neighbor is ill, do I reach out with comfort and concern?

Am I too concerned with my own needs to see the needs of those who may be sick in body, mind, or spirit?

Am I willing to share my own faith with one who lacks faith?

"I was in prison and you visited me."

When I meet someone who is imprisoned in worlds of addiction, do I offer help and consolation?

When I myself am imprisoned by my own sin, do I seek the forgiveness of God through the celebration of the sacraments?

PRAYER OF BLESSING FOR A PARISH MEAL DURING ADVENT

O God our creator,
we ask for your blessing on the food
and the friendships we share.
As we wait in joyful hope
for the coming of your Son,
keep us mindful of those who have nothing to eat.
Inspire us to work to bring food to the hungry,
shelter to the homeless,
and hope to those who despair.
Bless those who have prepared this meal,
and bless us as we enjoy the abundance
of your gifts of food and drink.
We ask this through Christ our Lord. Amen.

PRAYER OF BLESSING FOR A PARISH MEAL DURING THE CHRISTMAS SEASON

O God of wonder,

you sent your Son, Jesus,

as a blessing upon all who dwell upon the earth.

Send your blessing upon the food we are about to share,

on those who provided it for us,

and upon those who prepared it.

As we enjoy this meal,

keep us mindful of those who have nothing to eat.

May the sharing of this meal

renew our efforts to bring the good news to the poor.

We ask this through Christ our Lord. Amen.

PRAYER OF BLESSING FOR A PARISH MEAL DURING LENT

O God of mercy and compassion,
with humility of heart
we ask your blessing on the meal we are about to share.
During this season of prayer, fasting, and almsgiving
may we be inspired to share our gifts with the needy.
May the sharing of this meal
urge us on to work tirelessly to bring your word of comfort
to all who seek meaning and direction in their lives.
Bless us, the food we are about to receive,
those who prepared it,
and the friendships we share.
We ask this in the name of your Son, Jesus Christ,
who is Lord forever and ever. Amen.

PRAYER OF BLESSING FOR A PARISH MEAL DURING A LENTEN SIMPLE MEAL

Merciful God,
we gather in this place to share a simple meal.
Let this meal remind us that
hundreds of millions of people across this planet
will go to sleep hungry this very night.
May our Lenten sacrifice
help those who are in need
in this community and beyond.
Bless this food,
those who have prepared this meal,
and those who will clean up when it is finished.
As we continue our Lenten journey,
keep our eyes fixed on the upcoming celebration
of the passion, death, and resurrection of your Son,
who is Lord forever and ever. Amen.

PRAYER OF BLESSING FOR A PARISH MEAL DURING THE EASTER SEASON

You shower us with blessings,
O God of love.
In this season of joy,
when we celebrate Christ's death and resurrection,
you continue to bless and protect us.
As we prepare to share this meal,
keep us mindful of those who this night will die of hunger.
As believers who have put on Christ in baptism,
make us bearers of gospel justice.
Bless this food and the friendships we share.
We ask this through Christ our Lord. Amen.

You give us every good gift,
O God of the covenant.
Help us to see in the food spread before us
another outpouring of your grace.
Be with us as we share this meal
and keep us ever mindful of the hungry.
Bless us and the food we are about to receive.
We ask this through Christ our Lord. Amen.

PRAYER SERVICES FOR PARISH LIFE © 2004, World Library Publications • 800-566-6150 • WLP 017264. All rights reserved.

Prayer Service for Baptism Preparation Sessions

If the prayer service takes place in a meeting room, the space should be prepared ahead of time. In a central location, a bowl of water should be placed on a table. The table may be adorned with flowers and candles. A baptismal garment and the vessels containing the oil of catechumens and the sacred chrism may also be place on the table. If the service takes place in church, the baptismal font should be used for the ritual that takes place after the liturgy of the word. The other baptismal symbols may be placed on a table near the font.

The leader invites all to rise.

The prayer service may begin with an appropriate song.

Leader: Brothers and sisters, we praise God for the miracle of new life. Each time a child is born into the human family, the face of God is revealed to the world. We rejoice with the angels and saints, who sing a song of joy at the upcoming baptism of those who will become the newest members of God's family. How wonderful that the people of God will be enriched by the addition of these little ones who will grow in God's love and who, one day, will be nourished by God's word and by the body and blood of Christ. Let us take time now to listen to God's word.

The leader invites all to be seated.

Reading of the Word of God

First Reading
1 Peter 2:4–5, 9–10

Beloved: Come to the Lord, a living stone, though rejected by mortals yet chosen and precious in God's sight, and like living stones, let yourselves be built into a spiritual house, to be a holy priesthood, to offer spiritual sacrifices acceptable to God through Jesus Christ.

You are a chosen race, a royal priesthood, a holy nation, God's own people, in order that you may proclaim the mighty acts of him who called you out of darkness into his marvelous light.

> Once you were not a people,
>   but now you are God's people;
> once you had not received mercy,
>   but now you have received mercy.

The word of the Lord.

Response
Psalm 23:1–6

Leader: **The LORD is my shepherd, I shall not want.**
He makes me lie down in green pastures;
he leads me beside still waters;
he restores my soul.

All: The LORD is my shepherd, I shall not want.
He makes me lie down in green pastures;
he leads me beside still waters;
he restores my soul.

Leader: **He leads me in right paths**
for his name's sake.
Even though I walk through the darkest valley,
I fear no evil;

All: For you are with me;
your rod and your staff—
they comfort me.

Leader: **You prepare a table before me**
in the presence of my enemies;

All: You anoint my head with oil;
my cup overflows.

Leader: **Surely goodness and mercy shall follow me**
all the days of my life;

All: And I shall dwell in the house of the LORD
my whole life long.

Leader: **The LORD is my shepherd, I shall not want.**
He makes me lie down in green pastures;
he leads me beside still waters;
he restores my soul.

All: The LORD is my shepherd, I shall not want.
He makes me lie down in green pastures;
he leads me beside still waters;
he restores my soul.

Gospel *(All rise.)*
Mark 10:13–16

People were bringing little children to Jesus in order that he might touch them; and the disciples spoke sternly to them. But when Jesus saw this, he was indignant and said to them, "Let the little children come to me; do not stop them; for it is to such as these that the kingdom of God belongs. Truly I tell you, whoever does not receive the kingdom of God as a little child will never enter it." And he took them up in his arms, laid his hands on them, and blessed them.

The Gospel of the Lord.

BAPTISMAL RECOMMITMENT

Leader: During the liturgy for baptism, we will be asked to make the profession of faith and baptismal promises for our children, who are not yet old enough to grasp the meaning of these promises. At that sacred moment in the ritual, we pledge that what we have become as baptized believers will be infused into the minds and hearts of our children. This is no simple task. When that moment arrives, remember the responsibility that comes with baptism. It is simply this: to become Christ for one another.

         As a sign of our willingness to share the faith and promises of our own baptism with our children, I would ask that each of you now come forward, dip your hand in this bowl of water (baptism font) and make the sign of the cross. As you perform this ancient gesture, remember that you will soon be asked to trace that cross on the forehead of those to be baptized. This is the very first sacramental gesture the Church uses as new members are welcomed. It is the cross that is the way for all Christians. As you sign yourself, pray that all will willingly embrace this cross, which brings pain and joy, struggle and victory.

The leader invites all to approach the vessel of water and make the sign of the cross.

INTERCESSIONS

Leader: Friends, let us now turn to God in our need. Let our response be "Lord, hear our prayer."

That those soon to be baptized will be blessed abundantly and always live as children of the light, we pray to the Lord. R/.

That parents will develop a deep respect for their responsibilities as Christian mothers and fathers, we pray to the Lord. R/.

That godparents will always be an example of Gospel virtue for their godchild, we pray to the Lord. R/.

That grandparents will be signs of wisdom in our families and examples of God's love and kindness to their grandchildren, we pray to the Lord. R/.

That we will all learn to appreciate the great gift and the responsibility that come with having been baptized into Christ Jesus, we pray to the Lord. R/.

Let us pray now in the words our Savior gave us. Our Father . . .

CLOSING PRAYER

Leader: Let us pray.
O God of wonder,
we praise and thank you
for this opportunity to come together in prayer.
You are the giver of every good gift.
We thank you for the gift of new life
that brings joy to the world.
Through the death and resurrection of your Son,
you bring life to your people.
You forgive our sins,
wash us clean,
and call us always to live as your faithful people.
Bless us as we seek to do your will,
and bring us all one day into the eternal happiness of heaven.
We ask this through Christ our Lord.

All: Amen.

Leader: To conclude our celebration, let us share a sign of Christ's peace with one another.

The prayer service may conclude with an appropriate song.

PRAYER SERVICES FOR PARISH LIFE © 2004, World Library Publications • 800-566-6150 • WLP 017264. Scripture quotations are from the New Revised Standard Version of the Bible © 1989 by the Division of Christian Education of the National Council of the Churches of Christ in the USA. All rights reserved. Used with permission.

Prayer Service for Engaged Couples Preparing for Marriage

In many parishes, engaged couples come together for a number of reasons: wedding ceremony planning, marriage preparation, and the administering of marriage inventories. This prayer service can assist in placing any of these activities in the context of prayer.

Before the service, an open Lectionary (or Bible) should be placed on a table near the center of the prayer space. This table may be adorned with flowers and candles.

The leader invites all to rise.

The prayer service may begin with an appropriate song.

Call to Worship

Leader: **Sisters and brothers, God has drawn you into each other's lives and given you the grace of love and companionship. We praise God for these gifts and ask God to nurture them. As you prepare to celebrate your wedding, look to God to be your strength and your guide. Let us lift our hearts and voices in prayer.**

All: God of everlasting love and truth,
thank you for a gift that is beyond measure:
the gift of the one with whom I will share the rest of my life.
Strengthen us as our relationship unfolds.
Do not let us forget that it is you who have drawn us together.
Help us always to recognize your presence in our marriage
and keep us always under your care and protection.
We ask this through Christ our Lord. Amen.

The leader invites all to be seated.

Reading of the Word of God

First Reading
Colossians 3:12–17

Brothers and sisters: As God's chosen ones, holy and beloved, clothe yourselves with compassion, kindness, humility, meekness, and patience. Bear with one another and, if anyone has a complaint against another, forgive each other; just as the Lord has forgiven you, so you also must forgive. Above all, clothe yourselves with love, which binds everything together in perfect harmony. And let the peace of Christ rule in your hearts, to which indeed you were called in the one body. And be thankful. Let the word of Christ dwell in you richly; teach and admonish one another in all wisdom; and with gratitude in your hearts sing psalms, hymns, and spiritual songs to God. And whatever you do, in word or deed, do everything in the name of the Lord Jesus, giving thanks to God the Father through him.
The word of the Lord.

Response
Psalm 103:1–2, 8, 13, 17–18a

Leader: **Bless the LORD, O my soul,
and all that is within me,
bless his holy name.**

All: Bless the LORD, O my soul,
and all that is within me
bless his holy name.

Leader: **Bless the LORD, O my soul,
and do not forget all his benefits.**

All: The LORD is merciful and gracious,
slow to anger and abounding in steadfast love.

Leader: **As a father has compassion for his children,
so the LORD has compassion for those who fear him.**

All: But the steadfast love of the LORD is from everlasting to everlasting
on those who fear him,
and his righteousness to children's children,
to those who keep his covenants
and remember to do his commandments.

Leader: **Bless the LORD, O my soul,
and all that is within me,
bless his holy name.**

All: Bless the LORD, O my soul,
and all that is within me,
bless his holy name.

Gospel *(All rise.)*
John 15:9–12

**Jesus said to his disciples, "As the Father has loved me, so I have loved you; abide in my love. If you keep my commandments, you will abide in my love, just as I have kept my Father's commandments and abide in his love. I have said these things to you so that my joy may be in you, and that your joy may be complete. "This is my commandment, that you love one another as I have loved you."
The Gospel of the Lord.**

PLEDGE OF COMMITMENT TO GOD'S WORD

The leader invites all to rise.

Leader: Brothers and sisters, God nourishes us through the sacred word throughout our lives. Whether we read the Bible as part of our personal prayer, are involved in Bible study groups, or gather with a believing assembly to hear God's word, this word sustains us in our relationships with our spouse, our children, and all those we meet. God's word is an active word, and the foundation of that activity, as we heard from John's Gospel, is love for one another. I invite each couple to come to the table upon which is enthroned the sacred word of God. As you come to the table, place your hands on that word, being sure to touch each other's hands as you do so, for God's word will bring your marriage peace, challenge, comfort, joy, and strength.

As each couple comes forward, they pace their hands on the Lectionary (or Bible). The leader invokes this blessing:

Leader: N. and N., this word will draw you into a closer relationship with each other and with God. May God's love deepen your love as you move closer to your wedding day.

Leader: Let us join our hearts together now and pray in the words that Jesus gave us. Our Father . . .

CLOSING PRAYER

Leader: Let us pray.
O God of light and love,
fill us with your peace.
As our love for one another grows,
keep us mindful that all good gifts come from you.
As the day of our commitment to one another approaches,
send us a spirit of courage and peace.
Help us to look beyond the details of our wedding
to discover the depth of the love
you have planted within our hearts.
We ask all of this through Christ our Lord.

All: Amen.

Leader: Friends, to conclude this prayer service, let us extend a sign of Christ's peace to one another.

The prayer service may conclude with an appropriate song.

SERVICE FOR CHRISTIAN UNITY

The leader invites all to rise.

The prayer service may begin with an appropriate song.

CALL TO PRAYER

Leader: **Come, let us return to the LORD; . . .**
he will heal us . . .
and he will bind us up. *Hosea 6:1*

All: Let us look to him, and be radiant;
that our faces shall never be ashamed. *Psalm 34:5*

Leader: **Let us express our faith as we pray the words handed down to us**
through Christian tradition as the Apostles' Creed.

All: I believe in God, the Father almighty,
> creator of heaven and earth.
I believe in Jesus Christ, his only Son, our Lord.
>> He was conceived by the power of the Holy Spirit
>>> and born of the Virgin Mary.
>> He suffered under Pontius Pilate,
>>> was crucified, died, and was buried.
>> He descended to the dead.
>> On the third day he rose again.
>> He ascended into heaven,
>>> and is seated at the right hand of the Father.
>> He will come again to judge the living and the dead.
I believe in the Holy Spirit,
> the holy catholic Church,
> the communion of saints,
> the forgiveness of sins,
> the resurrection of the body,
> and life everlasting. Amen.

The leader invites all to be seated.

READING OF THE WORD OF GOD

First Reading
Leviticus 26:3–4, 9, 12

If you follow my statutes and keep my commandments and observe them faithfully, I will give you your rains in their season, and the land shall yield its produce, and the trees of the field shall yield their fruit. I will look with favor upon you and make you fruitful and multiply you; and I will maintain my covenant with you. And I will walk among you, and will be your God, and you shall be my people. The word of the Lord.

Response
Jeremiah 31:10, 11–12ab, 13–14

Leader:	R/. Lord, gather your scattered people.
All:	R/. Lord, gather your scattered people.

Leader:	Hear the word of the LORD, O nations,
	        and declare it in the coastlands far away;
	say, "He who scattered Israel will gather him,
	        and will keep him as a shepherd a flock." R/.

Leader:	For the LORD has ransomed Jacob,
	        and has redeemed him from hands too strong for him.
	They shall come and sing aloud on the height of Zion,
	        and they shall be radiant over the goodness of the LORD. R/.

Leader:	Then shall the young women rejoice in the dance,
	        and the young men and the old shall be merry.
	I will turn their mourning into joy,
	        I will comfort them and give them gladness for sorrow. R/.

Second Reading
Ephesians 2:19–22

You are no longer strangers and aliens, but you are citizens with the saints and also members of the household of God, built upon the foundation of the apostles and prophets, with Christ Jesus himself as the cornerstone. In him the whole structure is joined together and grows into a holy temple in the Lord; in whom you also are built together spiritually into a dwelling place for God.

The word of the Lord.

Gospel *(All rise.)*
John 10:11–16

"I am the good shepherd. The good shepherd lays down his life for the sheep. The hired hand, who is not the shepherd and does not own the sheep, sees the wolf coming and leaves the sheep and runs away—and the wolf snatches them and scatters them. The hired hand runs away because a hired hand does not care for the sheep. I am the good shepherd. I know my own and my own know me, just as the Father knows me and I know the Father. And I lay down my life for the sheep. I have other sheep that do not belong to this fold. I must bring them also, and they will listen to my voice. So there will be one flock, one shepherd."

The Gospel of the Lord.

INTERCESSIONS

(based on Ephesians 4:5–6, 31–32)

Leader: **Hope for Christian unity begins with respect for one another. Let us pray for peace and harmony among all people.**

All: Father, may those divided by anger, fear, or misunderstanding see the truth and forgive one another.

Leader: **Let us pray for Christian unity.**

All: May we see the blessings of variety in our traditions and find unity in one Lord, one faith, one baptism, one God and Father.

We may add other intentions, with the response:

All: Lord, hear our prayer.

Leader: **Let us pray in the words our Savior taught us:**

All: Our Father . . .

BLESSING

Leader: **May the God of steadfastness and encouragement**
grant you to live in harmony with one another,
in accordance with Christ Jesus,
so that together you may with one voice
glorify the God and Father of our Lord Jesus Christ.   *Romans 15:5–6*

All: Amen.

The prayer service may conclude with an appropriate song.

PRAYER SERVICES FOR PARISH LIFE © 2004, World Library Publications • 800-566-6150 • WLP 017264. Scripture quotations are from the New Revised Standard Version of the Bible © 1989 by the Division of Christian Education of the National Council of the Churches of Christ in the USA. All rights reserved. Used with permission.

Lenten Service Based on the Final Words of Christ

The leader invites all to rise.

The prayer service may begin with an appropriate song.

Call to Celebration

Leader:	**Draw near to God, and he will draw near to you.**	*James 4:8*
All:	Hear my cry, O God;	
	listen to my prayer.	*Psalm 61:1*

Opening Prayer

Leader: **Let us pray.**

Lord Jesus Christ, our Redeemer,
we confidently gather around your cross.
We ask mercy for ourselves and all those for whom we pray.
Grant us the light and strength to know you and love you,
to be sorry for our sins, and to serve you in one another.

We ask this in your holy name, our Redeemer forever and ever.

All: Amen.

The leader invites all to be seated.

Reading of the Word of God

I

Luke 23:32–34

Two others also, who were criminals, were led away to be put to death with Jesus. When they came to the place that is called The Skull, they crucified Jesus there with the criminals, one on his right and one on his left. Then Jesus said,

All: "Father, forgive them; for they do not know what they are doing."

Silent prayer, reflective music, or meditative comment may follow.

Leader: **Have mercy on us, O Lord.**

All: Jesus, we believe in you, we hope in you, we love you.
Through your cross you brought us the hope of resurrection.

II

Luke 23:39–43

One of the criminals who were hanged there kept deriding him and saying, "Are you not the Messiah? Save yourself and us!" But the other rebuked him, saying, "Do you not fear God, since you are under the same sentence of condemnation? And we indeed have been condemned justly, for we are getting what we deserve for our deeds, but this man has done nothing wrong." Then he said, "Jesus, remember me when you come into your kingdom." He replied,

All: "Truly I tell you, today you will be with me in Paradise."

Silent prayer, reflective music, or meditative comment may follow.

Leader: **Have mercy on us, O Lord.**

All: Jesus, we believe in you, we hope in you, we love you.
Through your cross you brought us the hope of resurrection.

III

John 19:25–27

Standing near the cross of Jesus were his mother, and his mother's sister, Mary the wife of Clopas, and Mary Magdalene. When Jesus saw his mother and the disciple whom he loved standing beside her, he said to his mother,

All: "Woman, here is your son."

Leader: **Then he said to the disciple,**

All: "Here is your mother."

Silent prayer, reflective music, or meditative comment may follow.

Leader: **Have mercy on us, O Lord.**

All: Jesus, we believe in you, we hope in you, we love you.
Through your cross you brought us the hope of resurrection.

IV

Matthew 27:45–46

From noon on, darkness came over the whole land until three in the afternoon. And about three o'clock Jesus cried with a loud voice,

All: "My God, my God, why have you forsaken me?"

Silent prayer, reflective music, or meditative comment may follow.

Leader: **Have mercy on us, O Lord.**

All: Jesus, we believe in you, we hope in you, we love you.
Through your cross you brought us the hope of resurrection.

V

John 19:28

When Jesus knew that all was now finished, he said (in order to fulfill the scripture),

All: "I am thirsty."

Silent prayer, reflective music, or meditative comment may follow.

Leader: **Have mercy on us, O Lord.**

All: Jesus, we believe in you, we hope in you, we love you.
             Through your cross you brought us the hope of resurrection.

VI

John 19:29–30

A jar full of sour wine was standing there. So they put a sponge full of the wine on a branch of hyssop and held it to his mouth. When Jesus had received the wine, he said,

All: "It is finished."

Silent prayer, reflective music, or meditative comment may follow.

Leader: **Have mercy on us, O Lord.**

All: Jesus, we believe in you, we hope in you, we love you.
             Through your cross you brought us the hope of resurrection.

VII

Luke 23:44–46

It was now about noon, and darkness came over the whole land until three in the afternoon, while the sun's light failed; and the curtain of the temple was torn in two. Then Jesus, crying with a loud voice, said,

All: "Father, into your hands I commend my spirit."

Silent prayer, reflective music, or meditative comment may follow.

Leader: **Have mercy on us, O Lord.**

All: Jesus, we believe in you, we hope in you, we love you.
             Through your cross you brought us the hope of resurrection.

LITANY

Leader: **Please respond "Lord, save your people" to the following invocations.**

Jesus, Son of the living God, R/.

Jesus, Son of the sorrowing Mother, R/.

Jesus, light of the world, R/.

Jesus, burning with love for us, R/.

Jesus, abandoned by your disciples, R/.

Jesus, suffering on the cross, R/.

Jesus, obedient unto death, R/.

Jesus, rising to new life, R/.

Jesus, salvation of us all, R/.

Jesus, our peace and reconciliation, R/.

DISMISSAL

Leader: **"I will not leave you orphaned;
I am coming to you."**   *John 14:18*

All: Holy God, mighty God, ever-living God,
have mercy on us.

Leader: **Go in peace to serve the Lord in one another.**

All: Thanks be to God.

The prayer service may conclude with an appropriate song.

Blessing of Foods at Easter

This celebration occurs at a time of day when it is convenient for most to attend, so that they may share in its simple and beautiful teaching about the Resurrection. A red stole is appropriate if this service follows Good Friday's liturgy but precedes the introduction of white vestments at the Easter Vigil. This blessing might follow all Easter Masses.

Leader: **May the grace and peace of Jesus Christ be with you.**

All: And also with you.

Leader: **Friends, let us be attentive to the word of God.**

Reading of the Word of God

First Reading
Deuteronomy 26:1–5a, 10–11

When you have come into the land that the LORD your God is giving you as an inheritance to possess, and you possess it, and settle in it, you shall take some of the first of all the fruit of the ground, which you harvest from the land that the LORD your God is giving you, and you shall put it in a basket and go to the place that the LORD your God will choose as a dwelling for his name. You shall go to the priest who is in office at that time, and say to him, "Today I declare to the LORD your God that I have come into the land that the LORD swore to our ancestors to give us." When the priest takes the basket from your hand and sets it down before the altar of the LORD your God, you shall make this response before the LORD your God, "So now I bring the first of the fruit of the ground that you, O LORD, have given me." You shall set it down before the LORD your God and bow down before the LORD your God. Then you, together with the Levites and the aliens who reside among you, shall celebrate with all the bounty that the LORD your God has given to you and to your house.

The word of the Lord.

Response
Psalm 145

Leader: **I will extol you, my God and King,**
and bless your name forever and ever.
Every day I will bless you,
and praise your name forever and ever.
Great is the LORD, and greatly to be praised;
his greatness is unsearchable.

All: One generation shall laud your works to another,
and shall declare your mighty acts.
On the glorious splendor of your majesty,
and on your wondrous works, I will meditate.

Leader:	The might of your awesome deeds shall be proclaimed,
	and I will declare your greatness.
	They shall celebrate the fame of your abundant goodness,
	and shall sing aloud of your righteousness.
All:	The LORD is gracious and merciful,
	slow to anger and abounding in steadfast love.
	The LORD is good to all,
	and his compassion is over all that he has made.
Leader:	All your works shall give thanks to you, O LORD,
	and all your faithful shall bless you.
	They shall speak of the glory of your kingdom,
	and tell of your power,
	to make known to all people your mighty deeds,
	and the glorious splendor of your kingdom.
All:	Your kingdom is an everlasting kingdom,
	and your dominion endures throughout all generations.
	The LORD is faithful in all his words,
	and gracious in all his deeds.

Gospel *(All rise.)*
Matthew 7:7

Jesus said to his disciples, "Ask, and it will be given you; search, and you will find; knock, and the door will be opened for you. For everyone who asks receives, and everyone who searches finds, and for everyone who knocks, the door will be opened."

The Gospel of the Lord.

BLESSING

BLESSING OF THE PASCHAL LAMB

Leader:	We begin our blessings with the blessing of the paschal lamb. Father, giver of all good things, you commanded our ancestors in faith to partake of lamb on Passover night. ✠ Bless this lamb prepared for our celebration in honor of your Son's Passover from death to life, for he is truly the Paschal Lamb by whose blood we are saved. As we enjoy the food that you sanctify for our nourishment, may we also obtain your blessing through the cross and resurrection of your Son. Yours is the power, Father, Son, and Holy Spirit, now and forever.
All:	Amen.

BLESSING OF OTHER MEATS

Leader: Now, let us bless other meats.

O God, through Moses you commanded your people in their deliverance from Egypt to kill a lamb and mark the doorposts with its blood. We understand this to prefigure our deliverance by Jesus' shedding of his blood. May it please you to bless ✠ and sanctify this meat, which we desire to eat in praise of his name, our Paschal Lamb, who lives and reigns forever and ever.

All: Amen.

BLESSING OF BREAD

Leader: Now, let us bless bread.

Almighty, everlasting God, be pleased to bless ✠ this bread. May it be a healthful food for body and soul, a safeguard against every disease, and a defense against all harm. We ask this through our Lord Jesus Christ, the Bread of Life, who came down from heaven and gives life and salvation to all the world, who lives and reigns forever and ever.

All: Amen.

BLESSING OF DAIRY FOODS

Leader: Next, let us bless dairy foods.

O God, creator and author of all being, ✠ bless these cheeses, butter, and other dairy foods. Keep us in your love, so that as we partake of them, we may be filled with your bountiful gifts on account of our Lord's glorious resurrection from the dead. We give glory to you, our Father without beginning, to your Son who is our true Food, and to your good and life-giving Spirit, now and forever.

All: Amen.

BLESSING OF EGGS

Leader: Now let us bless eggs.

Father in heaven, let your blessing ✠ come upon these eggs. When we break them, we see a sign of your Son rising to new life from the tomb. May we eat them in joyful celebration of his resurrection, for he lives and reigns forever and ever.

All: Amen.

BLESSING OF CAKES AND PASTRIES

Leader: Now let us bless cakes and pastries.

Lord Jesus Christ, living bread of everlasting life, ✠ bless these cakes and pastries as you once blessed the five loaves in the wilderness. As we eat them may we receive the health we desire for body and soul. We ask this of you, our risen Lord, who lives and reigns forever and ever.

All: Amen.

BLESSING OF OTHER FOODS

Leader: Now let us bless all other foods.

O God, through Moses you directed the Israelites to carry their baskets to the priests for a blessing. Hear our prayers and shower abundant ✠ blessings on us and these assorted foods, which we gratefully present to you in honor of your Son's resurrection. Grant that we may find them a remedy against sickness, a source of strength for our bodies, and a protection of soul, by calling on your holy name. We ask this through Christ our Lord.

All: Amen.

BLESSING OF WINE

Leader: Now let us bless wine, the fruit of the vine.

Lord Jesus Christ, Son of the living God, in Cana of Galilee you changed water into wine. Be pleased to bless ✠ this wine, which you have given us as refreshment. Grant that whenever it is taken as drink, it may be accompanied by an outpouring of your life-giving grace, forever and ever.

All: Amen.

BLESSING OF CHILDREN AND THEIR EASTER BASKETS

Leader: We now bless all the children and their Easter baskets.

Loving Father, long ago you told your people to bring the good things for eating and celebrating to your altar in thanksgiving. They obeyed and brought you their baskets of food and grain before they ate and celebrated. Today these boys and girls do the same as they come here with their Easter baskets. We ask you to bless ✠ them and their parents and friends. Grant that they and their families may appreciate all that you give them. Bless ✠ their Easter eggs and candy and all that the baskets contain, with which they will celebrate the resurrection of Jesus, your Son and our brother. As they eat these foods and candies may their Easter joy increase. We ask this through Christ our Lord.

All: Amen.

Leader: Father, you graciously give us nourishment and strength for life's needs. We ask your blessing ✠ on our meal and on our companionship. Let us not eat to excess to displease you, and let not the sparkling wine tempt us to misdeeds. While we enjoy our feast, in charity let us also remember those who suffer hunger and want. Let not the pleasures of this life stifle the inspirations of your Holy Spirit. We ask this through Christ our Lord.

All: Amen.

The leader may sprinkle the foods and people with holy water.

CONCLUDING RITE

Leader: **This is the day the Lord has made.**

All: Let us rejoice and be glad.

Leader: **By faith we rose with Jesus in baptism.**

All: May we remain united with him forever.

Leader: **Go now in peace and may God bless you always.**

All: Amen.

The prayer service may conclude with an appropriate song.

CROWNING AN IMAGE OF THE BLESSED VIRGIN MARY

The leader invites all to rise.

The prayer service may begin with an appropriate song.

Leader: My friends,
in the glory of springtime
we give praise to our Lord Jesus Christ,
whose death, burial, and resurrection
have made all things new.
Today with great affection
we crown an image of Holy Mary,
the Mother of God and the Queen of heaven.
In faith she kept watch
near the cross of her Son Jesus.
She became the Mother of the Church,
a witness to the resurrection of the Lord.

OPENING PRAYER

Leader: Let us pray.

Gracious God,
after your Son Jesus ascended to you in glory,
his disciples gathered with his mother, Mary.
Together they devoted themselves to prayer
as they awaited the gift of your Holy Spirit.
Keep us also devoted to prayer,
of one heart and one mind,
in the good company of Holy Mary,
our Blessed Mother,
the Mother of all who have been reborn
in the waters of baptism.

We ask this through Christ our Lord.

All: Amen.

The leader invites all to be seated.

READING OF THE WORD OF GOD

Acts 1:12–14

The disciples returned to Jerusalem from the mount called Olivet, which is near Jerusalem, a sabbath day's journey away. When they had entered the city, they went to the room upstairs where they were staying, Peter, and John, and James, and Andrew, Philip and Thomas, Bartholomew and Matthew, James son of Alphaeus, and Simon the Zealot, and Judas son of James. All these were constantly devoting themselves to prayer, together with certain women, including Mary the mother of Jesus.

The word of the Lord.

Response

Leader:	**Mary gives us Jesus, the light of the world.**
All:	May he shine forth through us.
Leader:	**Mary gives us Jesus crucified.**
All:	May we die to our selfish inclinations.
Leader:	**Mary gives us Jesus, risen to new life.**
All:	May we rise with him to eternal glory.

Any appropriate Marian hymn may be sung.

The crowning may occur during the song.

LITANY OF MARY, MOTHER OF THE CHURCH

Leader:	**Lord, have mercy.**
All:	Lord, have mercy.
Leader:	**Christ, have mercy.**
All:	Christ, have mercy.
Leader:	**Lord, have mercy.**
All:	Lord, have mercy.
Leader:	**God our Father in heaven,**
All:	Have mercy on us.
Leader:	**God the Son, our Redeemer,**
All:	Have mercy on us.
Leader:	**God the Holy Spirit,**
All:	Have mercy on us.
Leader:	**Holy Trinity, one God,**
All:	Have mercy on us.
Leader:	**Please respond "pray for us" after each invocation.**
	Holy Mary,
All:	R/. Pray for us.

Leader:	Mother of God, R/.
	Woman of faith, R/.
	Most honored of all virgins, R/.
	Joy of Israel, R/.
	Honor of our people, R/.
	Model of prayer and virtue, R/.
	Incentive to trust, R/.
	Temple of the Holy Spirit, R/.
	Spouse of Joseph, R/.
	Mother of Jesus, R/.
	Faithful follower of Jesus, R/.
	Mother of the Church, R/.
	Image of the Church at prayer, R/.
	Our Lady of Guadalupe, patroness of the Americas, R/.
	Mary Immaculate, patroness of the United States, R/.
	Advocate of life, R/.
	Guide of the young, R/.
	Friend of the single, R/.
	Companion of the married, R/.
	Voice for the unborn, R/.
	Mother of mothers, R/.
	Support of the family, R/.
	Comforter of the sick, R/.
	Nurse of the aged, R/.
	Echo of the suffering, R/.
	Consoler of the widowed, R/.
	Strength of the brokenhearted, R/.
	Hymn of the joyful, R/.
	Hope of the poor, R/.
	Example of detachment for the rich, R/.
	Goal of pilgrims, R/.
	Resort of the traveler, R/.
	Protector of the exiled, R/.
	Woman most whole, R/.
	Virgin most free, R/.
	Wife most loving, R/.
	Mother most fulfilled, R/.
	Queen of love, R/.

Leader:	**Lamb of God, you take away the sins of the world:**
All:	Have mercy on us.
Leader:	**Lamb of God, you take away the sins of the world:**
All:	Have mercy on us.

Leader:	**Lamb of God, you take away the sins of the world:**
All:	Have mercy on us.
All:	Remember, O most loving Virgin Mary,
	that never was it known
	that anyone who fled to your protection,
	implored your help, or sought your intercession
	was left unaided.
	Inspired with this confidence, we turn to you,
	O Virgin of virgins, our Mother.
	To you we come, before you we stand,
	sinful and sorrowful.
	O Mother of the Word Incarnate,
	do not despise our petitions,
	but in your mercy hear and answer us.
	Amen.

BLESSING

Leader:	**Please respond "Amen" to each blessing prayer.**
	May Mary's pilgrimage of faith strengthen us
	in our individual Christian vocations.
All:	Amen.
Leader:	**May Mary's loving desire that her Son's words be heeded**
	hasten Christian unity.
All:	Amen.
Leader:	**May Mary's motherly intercession**
	make us worthy of Jesus' promises.
All:	Amen.
Leader:	**Mary is the daughter of God the Father,**
	Spouse of God the Holy Spirit,
	and Mother of God the Son.
	May the blessing of the Holy Trinity
	come upon us and remain with us forever.
All:	Amen.

The prayer service may conclude with an appropriate song.

BLESSING OF PETS

The prayer service may begin with an appropriate song.

Leader: In the beginning, when God created the heavens and the earth, animals were created to accompany human beings as helpers and partners. Today we come together to praise God for the gifts of our own helpers and partners—our pets. Each of us knows the importance of our pets. They provide companionship, protection, and comfort. They are a very real sign of God's creative presence among us. Let us be thankful for the gift of our pets.

OPENING PRAYER

Leader: Let us pray.

God of creation and everlasting goodness,
we gather together today with our pets,
your holy creatures that have become our guardians and companions.
Bless us this day
and keep us ever mindful
that you are the giver of every good gift.
We ask this through Christ our Lord.

All: Amen.

READING OF THE WORD OF GOD
Genesis 2:18–19

Then the LORD God said, "It is not good that the man should be alone; I will make him a helper as his partner." So out of the ground the LORD God formed every animal of the field and every bird of the air, and brought them to the man to see what he would call them; and whatever the man called every living creature, that was its name. The man gave names to all cattle, and to the birds of the air, and to every animal of the field.

The word of the Lord.

INTERCESSIONS

Leader: Let our response to these prayers be "Blessed be God forever."

Blessed be God, who created the world and found it very good. R/.

Blessed be God, who formed us out of the clay of the ground. R/.

Blessed be God, who created the animals to be our helpers. R/.

Blessed be God, who created horses, ponies, and donkeys. R/.

Blessed be God, who created poodles and pugs, beagles and bloodhounds, Dalmatians and dachshunds, and dogs of every mixed breed. R/.

Blessed be God, who created Siamese and Burmese, tabbies and tortoiseshells, Manx and Maine coons, and cats of every size and color. R/.

Blessed be God, who created hamsters and gerbils, ferrets and guinea pigs, rabbits and mice, and every kind of small pet. R/.

Blessed be God, who created parrots and parakeets, canaries and cockatoos, finches and pheasants, and every kind of tamed and wild bird. R/.

Blessed be God, who created frogs and toads, lizards and turtles, snakes and salamanders, and every kind of amphibian and reptile. R/.

Blessed be God, who created goldfish and angelfish, koi and clownfish, tetras and trout, and every kind of fish that swims in the seas, rivers, lakes, and aquariums. R/.

Blessed be God, who created pot-belly pigs and pinto ponies, owls and ocelots, alligators and anteaters, and every kind of unusual pet. R/.

Blessed be God, who created every kind of animal, and found them very good. R/.

BLESSING PRAYER

Leader: God our Creator, you made all things good.
In love look now on us and on our pets
and on all the creatures you have made.
As you once sent your angel Raphael
to guide your servant Tobiah and his faithful dog,
send your angel to watch over our pets.
Keep them in health and safety, secure in our care
to be our comfort and joy.
Remember them for life,
for you delight in life.
We ask this through Christ our Lord.

All: Amen.

The leader may then ask that each pet be brought forward for an individual blessing, or may sprinkle the pets with blessed water.

CONCLUDING RITE

Leader: **May God, who created the animals of the earth to be our helpers, continue to bless us now and always.**

All: Amen.

The prayer service may conclude with an appropriate song.

A Vigil Service Before Christmas

This service can suitably close the Advent season or be used as a prelude to one of the Masses of the Vigil of Christmas.

The prayer service may begin with an appropriate song: Lo, How a Rose E'er Blooming, People Look East, *or any appropriate song.*

I

The Great "O" Antiphons

Leader: During these past weeks we have been preparing to celebrate the Lord's coming. Today we know that he will come and in the morning we will see his glory. Now we recall the long centuries during which humanity longed for salvation. We relive that expectation as we sing an ancient Advent song.

The church lights are dimmed. An unlighted seven-branch candelabrum stands in a central location. One candle is lighted during the introduction to each verse of the song, beginning with the lowest candle on each side of the candelabrum; the top candle is the last to be lighted.

Leader: Jesus is Emmanuel, "God with us," promised when our first parents became exiles from God and captives of sin. Because we desire him among us, we sing: "O come, O come, Emmanuel!"

Song: O Come, O Come, Emmanuel, verse 1

Leader: Jesus is the Word of God and Wisdom of the Father for all eternity. We sing the praises of the One who existed before the world began: "Come, O Wisdom!"

Song: O Come, O Come, Emmanuel, verse 2

Leader: The Lord of might appeared in the flames of the burning bush on Mount Sinai. We ask God to make us worthy to enter the Promised Land. We cry out: "Come, O Lord of might."

Song: O Come, O Come, Emmanuel, verse 3

Leader: Jesus is the flower of Jesse's stem. No greater flower bloomed on the family tree of Jesse, King David's father. Jesus would become the tree of life that brings us salvation, and so we pray: "Come, O Branch of Jesse's stem!"

Song: O Come, O Come, Emmanuel, verse 4

Leader: Jesus is the key of David. He came to unlock the prison of death and release us from the bonds of sin. We are grateful that he gave us freedom as we sing: "Come, O Key of David!"

Song: *O Come, O Come, Emmanuel, verse 5*

Leader: Jesus is the daystar, the sun that brightens the world's darkness. We will see him in splendor when he comes again. On that day he will cheer us, and so we sing: "Come, O Daystar!"

Song: *O Come, O Come, Emmanuel, verse 6*

Leader: Jesus is the Desired One of the nations, who unites us into one family. He was foretold as King and Prince of Peace. We his people sing: "O Come, Desire of Nations!"

Song: *O Come, O Come, Emmanuel, verse 7*

A choral/congregational program of carols may follow, and the service may conclude with the Posada procession.

II

THE POSADA PROCESSION

The crib scene has been prepared without the figures of Jesus, Mary, and Joseph. It is now illuminated. The following ceremony is based on the Hispanic custom of the posada (inn) procession searching for a place of shelter and rest.

Leader: During the past weeks we have been preparing to celebrate the Lord's coming. Today we know that he will come and in the morning we shall see his glory.

Song: *O Little Town of Bethlehem, verse 1*

The presiding minister and other ministers go in procession to a side entrance of the church. After the first verse there is silence, and a knock is sounded at that door. A person there may engage in this dialogue with the people.

Joseph: In the name of heaven, good friends, give us a place to stay this night.

All: This is not an inn; keep going. We don't open to strangers.

Song: *O Little Town of Bethlehem, verse 2*

During the song's second verse, the procession moves to another side entrance. The knocking occurs again, followed by this dialogue:

Joseph: I am Joseph, the carpenter from Nazareth. Do not refuse us, that God may reward you.

All: We don't care who you are; let us sleep. We already told you we won't let you in.

Song: *O Little Town of Bethlehem, verse 3*

During the third verse, the procession moves to the main entrance. The knocking occurs again, followed by this dialogue:

Joseph: My beloved wife, Mary, can go no farther. She is heaven's Queen who will bear God's Son.

All: Enter, holy pilgrims; you may use this poor place. Our houses and our hearts are open to you.

Song: *O Little Town of Bethlehem, verse 4*

The presiding minister opens the door to admit Mary and Joseph. During the singing of the fourth verse, representatives of parish organizations or children accompany the procession to the crib scene, carrying the figures of Jesus, Mary, and Joseph for placement there.

Song: *Silent Night* or *O Come, Little Children* or any appropriate song

The Christmas crib may be blessed at this time.

PRAYER SERVICE BEFORE ELECTIONS

The leader ivites all to rise.

The prayer service may begin with an appropriate song.

CALL TO WORSHIP

Leader: **O God, open our eyes.**

All: That we may see the way of truth.

Leader: **O Lord, keep us from all selfish intent.**

All: And hear us when we call on you.

OPENING PRAYER

Leader: **Let us pray.**

All-knowing God,
we gather to hear your word
and to pray for your guidance as we approach the time
to elect those who will next serve the nation in public office.
Enlighten our minds with understanding and perception
that we may continue to discover your truth.
Endow our wills with the strength to strive for justice.
Fill our hearts with love for the peace you alone give,
that we may be at peace with one another.
May our individual lives serve the good
of all the people of our land and beyond its shores.
We ask this through Christ our Lord.

All: Amen.

The leader invites all to be seated.

READING OF THE WORD OF GOD

First Reading
Exodus 18:20–22, 24; Deuteronomy 1:16–17

Jethro said to his son-in-law Moses, "Teach the people the statutes and instructions and make known to them the way they are to go and the things they are to do. You should also look for able men among all the people, men who fear God, are trustworthy, and hate dishonest gain; set such men over them as officers over thousands, hundreds, fifties and tens. Let them sit as judges for the people at all times; let them bring every important case to you, but decide every minor case themselves."

So Moses listened to his father-in-law and did all that he had said.

Moses charged the judges: "Give the members of your community a fair hearing, and judge rightly between one person and another, whether citizen or resident alien. You must not be partial in judging: hear out the small and the great alike; you shall not be intimidated by anyone, for the judgment is God's."

The word of the Lord.

Response
Psalm 72:1–2, 3–4ab, 7–8, 12–13, 17

Leader:	**In his days may righteousness flourish and peace abound, until the moon is no more.**
All:	In his days may righteousness flourish and peace abound, until the moon is no more.
Leader:	**Give the king your justice, O God, and your righteousness to a king's son. May he judge your people with righteousness, and your poor with justice.**
All:	May the mountains yield prosperity for the people, and the hills, in righteousness. May he defend the cause of the poor of the people, give deliverance to the needy, and crush the oppressor.
Leader:	**In his days may righteousness flourish, and peace abound until the moon is no more. May he have dominion from sea to sea, and from the River to the ends of the earth.**
All:	For he delivers the needy when they call, the poor and those who have no helper. He has pity on the weak and the needy, and saves the lives of the needy.

Leader:	May his name endure forever,
	his fame continue as long as the sun.
	May all nations be blessed in him;
	may they pronounce him happy.

Second Reading
2 Chronicles 19:4–6; 9

Jehoshaphat resided at Jerusalem; then he went out again among the people, from Beer-sheeba to the hill country of Ephraim, and brought them back to the LORD, the God of their ancestors. He appointed judges in the land in all the fortified cities of Judah, city by city, and said to the judges, "Consider what you are doing, for you judge not on behalf of human beings but on the LORD's behalf; he is with you in giving judgment.

He charged them, "This is how you shall act: in the fear of the LORD, in faithfulness, and with your whole heart."

The word of the Lord.

INTERCESSIONS

Leader:	We conclude our service with prayer for God's help.
	That love for justice may prevail in our elections, we pray to the Lord.
All:	R/. Lord, hear us and lead us to justice.
Leader:	That all voters may exercise their right to vote, we pray to the Lord. R/.
	That the news media may report the complete truth, we pray to the Lord. R/.
	That election judges and poll watchers may be honest, we pray to the Lord. R/.
	For wisdom and courage in elected officials, we pray to the Lord. R/.
	For peace and justice, at home and abroad, we pray to the Lord. R/.

Other intentions may be added.

Leader: Lord of all, both governed and governing,
let us love all that is just and life-giving.
Instill in us the desire for your glory
and the well-being of all people.
Help us in our deliberations
to find candidates of honor and integrity.
May our leaders, judges, and all public servants
be worthy stewards of peace and freedom.
We ask this through Christ our Lord.

All: Amen.

CONCLUSION

Leader: The peace of God be with us.
May God guide our deliberations with the light of holy wisdom
as we decide on suitable representatives in government.

All: Thanks be to God.

PRAYER SERVICES FOR PARISH LIFE © 2004, World Library Publications • 800-566-6150 • WLP 017264. Scripture quotations are from the New Revised Standard Version of the Bible © 1989 by the Division of Christian Education of the National Council of the Churches of Christ in the USA. All rights reserved. Used with permission.

PRAYER SERVICE FOR INDEPENDENCE DAY

The prayer service may begin with an appropriate song.

OPENING PRAYER

Leader: Let us pray.

            Almighty, everlasting God, the Ruler of all nations,
hear us as we gather around our flag
to celebrate liberty and justice for all.
May it remind us of the love
we owe to our country and all our fellow citizens,
of fidelity to our national ideals,
and of the desired unity of all people.
When we see our flag stand out in the breeze,
may it move our hearts to rededication to the common good.
May we always walk worthy of the ideals
of our colors and our country.
We pray in your holy name.

All: Amen.

READING OF THE WORD OF GOD
Psalm 9:1–2, 9–10

I will give thanks to the LORD with my whole heart;
     I will tell of all your wonderful deeds.
I will be glad and exult in you;
     I will sing praise to your name, O Most High.
The LORD is a stronghold for the oppressed,
     a stronghold in times of trouble.
And those who know your name put their trust in you,
     for you, O LORD, have not forsaken those who seek you.
The word of the Lord.

Response
America the Beautiful or any appropriate song

Second Reading
Isaiah 32:16–18

Then justice will dwell in the wilderness,
and righteousness abide in the fruitful field.
The effect of righteousness will be peace,
and the result of righteousness, quietness and trust forever.
My people will abide in a peaceful habitation,
in secure dwellings and in quiet resting places.

The word of the Lord.

Response *(inspired by Abraham Lincoln's Second Inaugural Address)*

Leader:	With malice toward none, with charity for all,
All:	R/. The fruit of righteousness is sown in peace.
Leader:	With firmness in the right, as God gives us to see the right, R/.
Leader:	Let us strive to finish the work we are in, to bind up the nation's wounds, R/.
Leader:	To care for him who shall have borne the battle and his widow and orphan, R/.
Leader:	To do all which may achieve and cherish a just and lasting peace among ourselves and with all nations. R/.

A public leader may address the assembly. In lieu of an address there may be some other manifestation of civic pride, such as a fireworks display where authorized, a patriotic musical performance, an artillery salute, or the raising or posting of the flag.

RESOLUTION

Leader:	Will you foster peace within our country and good will among all people?
All:	We will.
Leader:	Will you stand up for justice by keeping our laws and fulfilling the divine law of love?
All:	We will.
Leader:	Will you labor to enrich our land with your God-given talents, curing its ills and cherishing life in all its forms?
All:	We will.

LITANY OF PETITION

Leader: Let us pray for our country,
that it may be a blessing to the world.

Let our response be "Lord, hear our prayer."

Let us pray for our president, the members of Congress,
our governor, and all who serve us in public office: R/.

Let us pray for sound government and just laws,
good education, and justice at all levels of society: R/.

Let us pray for all the citizens of our country,
for the removal of all hatred, prejudice, and contempt
for those not of our color, class, or creed: R/.

Let us pray for peace and understanding among all people,
for the day when war will be no more
and all will be truly free in their human dignity and rights: R/.

Let us pray for all those who serve us,
especially in the search for ways to better the quality of life: R/.

Let us pray for the proper use of freedom,
especially in using our natural resources: R/.

CLOSING PRAYER

Leader: Let us pray.
Heavenly Father,
you have given us this good land for our heritage.
Enlighten us, that we may always provide a haven
for all who seek freedom and justice.
Defend our liberties, and fashion into one united people
the multitude brought here at different times
out of many nations and tongues.
Sustain us as we strive today to renew the freedoms
achieved at so great a price.
As we work to harness nature's resources
for the good of all,
keep us from violence and discord, pride and arrogance.
Guide us along the path of justice
which righteous, honorable men and women
have walked before us.
We ask this in your name, God, forever and ever.

All: Amen.

DISMISSAL

Leader: **Go forth in peace and freedom, renewed in spirit
to make our promised land of yesteryear
a true home for today and a sanctuary for all future generations.**

All: Amen.

The prayer service may conclude with an appropriate song.

PRAYER SERVICE FOR PEACE BASED ON THE WORDS OF SAINT FRANCIS OF ASSISI

The leader invites all to rise.

The prayer service may begin with an appropriate song.

Leader: Experiencing conflict, discord, and struggle, we say with Jeremiah, " 'Peace, peace,' when there is no peace." *(6:14)* This service seeks to recognize that sin frustrates God's plan for peace. We may begin to realize peace when we try to accomplish what Dante said long ago: "In God's will is our peace." In that spirit we pray: "O God, let there be peace, and let it begin with me."

CALL TO WORSHIP
Matthew 5:9

Leader: Blessed are the peacemakers;
for they will be called children of God.

All: Lord, make me an instrument of your peace.

OPENING PRAYER

Leader: Let us pray.
O God of peace,
our lives are torn by war,
our own private battles, and great world conflicts.
Our presence here shows our desire to be peaceful people.
Strengthen our efforts to live in harmony,
loving one another in peace.
We ask this through Christ our Lord.

All: Amen.

The leader invites all to be seated.

READING OF THE WORD OF GOD

First Reading
Isaiah 2:1–5

The word that Isaiah son of Amoz saw concerning Judah and Jerusalem.
> In days to come
> > the mountain of the LORD's house
> shall be established as the highest of the mountains,
> > and shall be raised above the hills;
> all the nations shall stream to it.
> > Many people shall come and say,
> "Come, let us go up to the mountain of the LORD,
> > to the house of the God of Jacob;
> that he may teach us his ways
> > and that we may walk in his paths."
> For out of Zion shall go forth instruction,
> > and the word of the LORD from Jerusalem.
> He shall judge between the nations,
> > and shall arbitrate for many peoples;
> they shall beat their swords into plowshares,
> > and their spears into pruning hooks;
> nation shall not lift up sword against nation,
> > neither shall they learn war any more.

> O house of Jacob,
> > come, let us walk
> > in the light of the LORD!

The word of the Lord.

Response
Psalm 122:6–8

All: Pray for the peace of Jerusalem:
> > "May they prosper who love you.
> Peace be within your walls,
> > and security within your towers."
> For the sake of my relatives and friends
> > I will say, "Peace be within you."

Second Reading
Philippians 4:6–9

Do not worry about anything, but in everything by prayer and supplication with thanksgiving let your requests be made known to God. And the peace of God, which surpasses all understanding, will guard your hearts and your minds in Christ Jesus.

Finally, beloved, whatever is true, whatever is honorable, whatever is just, whatever is pure, whatever is pleasing, whatever is commendable, if there is any excellence and if there is anything worthy of praise, think about these things. Keep on doing the things that you have learned and received and heard and seen in me, and the God of peace will be with you.

The word of the Lord.

Response
Colossians 1:19–20

All: In Christ Jesus all the fullness of God
was pleased to dwell,
and through him God was pleased
to reconcile to himself all things,
whether on earth or in heaven,
by making peace through the blood of his cross.

The leader invites all to rise.

RESOLUTION

Leader: **Peace I leave with you;
my peace I give to you.** *John 14:27*

All: Lord, make me an instrument of your peace.

Leader: **Do not be overcome by evil,
but overcome evil with good.** *Romans 12:21*

All: Where there is hatred, let me sow love.

Leader: **Father, forgive them;
for they do not know what they are doing.** *Luke 23:34*

All: Where there is injury, let me sow pardon.

Leader: **Do not doubt but believe.** *John 20:27*

All: Where there is doubt, let me sow faith.

Leader: **Hope does not disappoint us,
because God's love has been poured into our hearts
through the Holy Spirit
that has been given to us.** *Romans 5:5*

All: Where there is despair, let me sow hope.

Leader:	**You are the light of the world.**
	In the same way, let your light shine before others,
	so that they may see your good works
	and give glory to your Father in heaven. *Matthew 5:14, 16*
All:	Where there is darkness, let me sow light.
Leader:	**You will weep and mourn,**
	but the world will rejoice;
	you will have pain,
	but your pain will turn into joy. *John 16:20*
All:	Where there is sadness, let me sow joy.
Leader:	**God consoles us in all our affliction,**
	so that we may be able to console those
	who are in any affliction with the consolation
	with which we ourselves
	are consoled by God. *2 Corinthians 1:4*
All:	Divine Master, grant that I may not
	so much seek to be consoled as to console.
Leader:	**With all wisdom and insight**
	he has made known to us
	the mystery of his will,
	according to his good pleasure
	that he set forth in Christ. *Ephesians 1:8–9*
All:	Grant that I may not so much seek to be understood
	as to understand.
Leader:	**If I speak in the tongues of mortals and of angels,**
	but do not have love,
	I am a noisy gong or a clanging cymbal. *1 Corinthians 13:1*
All:	Grant that I may not so much seek to be loved
	as to love.
Leader:	**For those who want to save their life will lose it,**
	and those who lose their life for my sake
	will save it. *Luke 9:24*
All:	It is in giving that we receive.
Leader:	**Forgive us our debts**
	as we also have forgiven our debtors. *Mark 6:12*
All:	It is in pardoning that we are pardoned.

Leader: **Unless a grain of wheat falls into the earth and dies,
it remains just a single grain;
but if it dies, it bears much fruit.**

John 12:24

All: It is in dying that we are born to eternal life.

BLESSING

Leader: **May God the Father and the Lord Jesus Christ
grant us peace, love, and faith.**

All: Grace be with all
who love our Lord Jesus Christ with unfailing love.

The prayer service may conclude with an appropriate song.

PRAYER SERVICES FOR PARISH LIFE © 2004, World Library Publications • 800-566-6150 • WLP 017264. Scripture quotations are from the New Revised Standard Version of the Bible © 1989 by the Division of Christian Education of the National Council of the Churches of Christ in the USA. All rights reserved. Used with permission.

SERVICE OF PRAYER FOR PEACE

The leader invites all to rise.

The prayer service may begin with an appropriate song.

GREETING

Leader: In the name of the Father, ✠ and of the Son, and of the Holy Spirit.

All: Amen.

Leader: May abundant grace and the abiding peace of God be with you all.

All: And also with you.

Leader: Dear friends, we gather this day/night to bring our fears and concerns before God. In this time of strife, when terror grips the hearts of many, we take the time to ask the God of peace to bring peace to this earth. As we listen to the living word of God, let us pray that peace will begin right here, in our hearts, within this holy place, and that the power of our prayer will help peace spread throughout the world. Let us now pause in silent prayer.

OPENING PRAYER

Leader: Let us pray.
God of peace,
in this time of turmoil,
we turn to you with hearts longing for peace.
As fear grips us,
we ask for your blessed assurance.
Keep us close to your Son,
whose first Easter greeting was one of peace.
We ask this in his name, the Prince of Peace,
who is Lord forever and ever.

All: Amen.

The leader invites all to be seated.

READING OF THE WORD OF GOD

First Reading
Isaiah 11:1–10

A shoot shall come out from the stump of Jesse,
 and a branch shall grow out of his roots.
The spirit of the LORD shall rest on him,
  the spirit of wisdom and understanding,
  the spirit of counsel and might,
  the spirit of knowledge and the fear of the LORD.
His delight shall be in the fear of the LORD.

He shall not judge by what his eyes see,
 or decide by what his ears hear;
but with righteousness he shall judge the poor,
 and decide with equity for the meek of the earth;
he shall strike the earth with the rod of his mouth,
 and with the breath of his lips he shall kill the wicked.
Righteousness shall be the belt around his waist,
 and faithfulness the belt around his loins.

The wolf shall live with the lamb,
 the leopard shall lie down with the kid,
the calf and the lion and the fatling together,
 and a little child shall lead them.
The cow and the bear shall graze,
 their young shall lie down together;
 and the lion shall eat straw like the ox.
The nursing child shall play over the hole of the asp,
 and the weaned child shall put its hand on the adder's den.
They will not hurt or destroy
 on all my holy mountain;
for the earth will be full of the knowledge of the LORD
 as the waters cover the sea.

The word of the Lord.

Response
Psalm 72:1–7, 12–14

Leader: **In his days may righteousness flourish
  and peace abound, until the moon is no more.**

All: Give the king your justice, O God,
  and your righteousness to a king's son.
 May he judge your people with righteousness,
  and your poor with justice.

Leader:	May the mountains yield prosperity for the people,
	and the hills, in righteousness.
	May he defend the cause of the poor of the people,
	give deliverance to the needy,
	and crush the oppressor.
All:	May he live while the sun endures,
	and as long as the moon, throughout all generations.
	May he be like rain that falls on the mown grass,
	like showers that water the earth.
Leader:	For he delivers the needy when they call,
	the poor and those who have no helper.
	He has pity on the weak and the needy,
	and saves the lives of the needy.
All:	From oppression and violence he redeems their life;
	and precious is their blood in his sight.
	In his days may righteousness flourish
	and peace abound, until the moon is no more.

Gospel *(All rise.)*
John 20:19–23

When it was evening on that day, the first day of the week, and the doors of the house where the disciples had met were locked for fear of the Jews, Jesus came and stood among them and said, "Peace be with you." After he said this, he showed them his hands and his side. Then the disciples rejoiced when they saw the Lord. Jesus said to them again, "Peace be with you. As the Father has sent me, so I send you." When he had said this, he breathed on them and said to them, "Receive the Holy Spirit. If you forgive the sins of any, they are forgive them; if you retain the sins of any, they are retained."

The Gospel of the Lord.

INTERCESSIONS

Leader: **Let us turn to God in this time of need. God always hears the prayer of those who cry out in humility. As wars rage around this planet, we place our trust in God, the source of peace and justice.**

Reader: That the Church will never shrink away its obligation to preach the gospel of Jesus Christ, we pray to the Lord.

That those who lead nations will find peaceful solutions to disagreements over borders, religious preference, or ethnic diversity, we pray to the Lord.

That the people of _____, and all places in our world currently experiencing war, will soon know the peace of God's holy mountain, we pray to the Lord.

That we will face the challenge of the gospel to love our enemies and do good to those who persecute us, we pray to the Lord.

Let us pause now in silence to pray for our enemies . . . *(allow significant time for silence)* . . . that we will work together to break down barriers that divide, we pray to the Lord.

Let us pause now in silence to pray for the victims of war and injustice . . . *(allow significant time for silence)* . . . that they will be welcomed into the eternal peace of heaven, we pray to the Lord.

Finally, let us pause in silence to pray for peace in our world, our country, our neighborhoods, our church, our families, and in our hearts . . . *(allow significant time for silence)* . . . that the reign of peace inaugurated by Christ's coming will take root and flourish, we pray to the Lord.

Leader: Let us gather all our prayers into one by praying the words that the Lord Jesus, the giver of peace, taught us. Our Father . . .

CLOSING PRAYER

Leader: Let us pray.
O God of love and tender mercy,
your people cry out to you in time of strife.
We fear for the safety of those we love;
the miles that separate family members
cause us to worry.
Comfort us in our time of need.
We suffer with those whose lives are destroyed by war.
May our efforts aid and encourage them.
We long for the reign of peace promised by your Son.
Bring that peace to earth again.
May we never grow complacent, O God;
may we never see the world's wars as events that do not affect us,
for we know that we are all your children,
entrusted with preserving this fragile earth as a place of harmony, peace, and justice.
Hear our prayer, which we voice in the name of your Son, Jesus Christ, who is Lord forever and ever.

All: Amen.

BLESSING AND DISMISSAL

Leader: May God's peace, which is beyond all understanding, descend upon us and enter our hearts and the hearts of all. In the name of the Father, and of the Son, ✠ and of the Holy Spirit.

All: Amen.

Leader: To conclude this service of prayer, let us turn to one another and share a sign of Christ's peace.

The prayer service may conclude with an appropriate song.

PRAYER SERVICES FOR PARISH LIFE © 2004, World Library Publications • 800-566-6150 • WLP 017264. Scripture quotations are from the New Revised Standard Version of the Bible © 1989 by the Division of Christian Education of the National Council of the Churches of Christ in the USA. All rights reserved. Used with permission.

PRAYER SERVICE FOR COMFORT IN TIME OF DISASTER

This prayer service may be prayed in times of natural disaster, a catastrophic event in which many lives are lost, acts of terrorism, or any event that calls for prayer of comfort.

The leader invites all to rise.

The prayer service may begin with an appropriate song.

Leader:	Dear friends, we are gathered together to seek comfort and strength from God. It is natural for us to ask for God's assistance during this time of extreme grief and pain. We raise our voices in lament to God in our sadness and confusion. We raise our voices in prayer for those who have lost their lives. We raise our voices in pleading to God for those who must now walk the long road of healing. We raise our voices in concern to God for those who are now suffering the loss of their loved ones. We raise our voices in confidence to our God, whose care for us knows no end, even in the midst of tragedy. And we raise our voices in supplication to our God, asking for protection from further harm.

OPENING PRAYER

Leader:	Let us pray. O God of consolation, we stand before you stunned and dazed by the tragedies that have unfolded in these days. Hear the prayer of lament your people raise to you as we plead, "Why?" You are all-giving. You are all-loving. Your people are in pain. Send your spirit of comfort among us and bring us one day to healing. We ask this in the name of the one who consoled Martha and Mary at the death of their brother, Lazarus, Jesus Christ, your Son, who is Lord forever and ever.
All:	Amen.

The leader invites all to be seated.

First Reading
Lamentations 3:17–26

My soul is bereft of peace;
      I have forgotten what happiness is;
so I say, "Gone is my glory,
      and all that I had hoped for from the LORD.
The thought of my affliction and my homelessness
      is wormwood and gall!
My soul continually thinks of it
      and is bowed down within me.
But this I call to mind,
      and therefore I have hope:
The steadfast love of the LORD never ceases,
      his mercies never come to an end;
they are new every morning;
      great is your faithfulness.
"The LORD is my portion," says my soul,
      "therefore I will hope in him."
The LORD is good to those who wait for him,
      to the soul that seeks him.
It is good that one should wait quietly
      for the salvation of the LORD.

The word of the Lord.

or

Romans 8:31b–39

If God is for us, who is against us? He who did not withhold his own Son, but gave him up for all of us, will he not with him also give us everything else? Who will bring any charge against God's elect? It is God who justifies. Who is to condemn? Is it Christ Jesus, who died, yes, who was raised, who is at the right hand of God, who indeed intercedes for us. Who will separate us from the love of Christ? Will hardship, or distress, or persecution, or famine, or nakedness, or peril, or sword? As it is written,

      "For your sake we are being killed all day long;
        we are accounted as sheep to be slaughtered."

No, in all these things we are more than conquerors through him who loved us. For I am convinced that neither death, nor life, nor angels, nor rulers, nor things present, nor things to come, nor powers, nor height, nor depth, nor anything else in all creation, will be able to separate us from the love of God in Christ Jesus our Lord.

The word of the Lord.

Response
Psalm 80:1–7, 14–19

Leader: **Give ear, O Shepherd of Israel,**
                 you who lead Joseph like a flock!
             You who are enthroned upon the cherubim, shine forth
                 before Ephraim and Benjamin and Manasseh.
             Stir up your might,
                 and come and save us!

All: Stir up your might,
                 and come and save us!
             Restore us, O God;
                 let your face shine, that we may be saved.

Leader: **Restore us, O God;**
                 let your face shine, that we may be saved.
             O LORD God of hosts,
                 how long will you be angry with your people's prayers?
             You have fed them with the bread of tears,
                 and given them tears to drink in full measure.

All: You have fed them with the bread of tears,
                 and given them tears to drink in full measure.
             You make us the scorn of our neighbors;
                 our enemies laugh among themselves.
             Restore us, O God of hosts;
                 let your face shine, that we may be saved.

Leader: **Restore us, O God of hosts;**
                 let your face shine, that we may be saved.
             Turn again, O God of hosts;
                 look down from heaven, and see;
             have regard for this vine,
                 the stock that your right hand has planted.
             They have burned it with fire, they have cut it down;
                 may they perish at the rebuke of your countenance.

All: They have burned it with fire, they have cut it down;
                 may they perish at the rebuke of your countenance.
             But let your hand be upon the one at your right hand,
                 the one whom you made strong for yourself.
             Then we will never turn back from you;
                 give us life, and we will call on your name.
             Restore us, O LORD God of hosts;
                 let your face shine, that we may be saved.

Gospel *(All rise.)*
John 11:17–28

When Jesus arrived at Bethany, he found that Lazarus had already been in the tomb four days. Now Bethany was near Jerusalem, some two miles away, and many of the Jews had come to Martha and Mary to console them about their brother. When Martha heard that Jesus was coming, she went and met him, while Mary stayed at home. Martha said to Jesus, "Lord, if you had been here, my brother would not have died. But even now I know that God will give you whatever you ask of him." Jesus said to her, "Your brother will rise again." Martha said to him, "I know that he will rise again in the resurrection on the last day." Jesus said to her, " I am the resurrection and the life. Those who believe in me, even though they die, will live, and everyone who lives and believes in me will never die. Do you believe this?" She said to him, "Yes, Lord, I believe that you are the Messiah, the Son of God, the one coming into the world."

The Gospel of the Lord.

The leader invites all to rise.

INTERCESSIONS

Leader:	**Like Martha in today's Gospel, we often entreat God, crying, "What if?" and "If only." Let us cry out to God now on behalf of all who have been affected by the tragedy of recent days.**
	O God, you are the giver of life;
All:	Grant eternal life to those who have died.
Leader:	**O God, you are the source of all truth;**
All:	Help us to know the truth of your care for us.
Leader:	**O God, you are the wellspring of healing;**
All:	Bring comfort and strength to all who have been injured.
Leader:	**O God, you are the fountain of consolation;**
All:	Console those who have lost loved ones.
Leader:	**O God, you alone have power over evil;**
All:	Lead all who would harm your people to a change of heart.
Leader:	**O God, you are Lord of heaven and earth;**
All:	Hear us in our need and answer our prayer.
Leader:	**Let us raise our eyes to heaven and pray for the coming of the kingdom as Jesus taught us. Our Father . . .**

CLOSING PRAYER

Leader: Let us pray.
O God of compassion,
your people are in pain.
Send your Holy Spirit among us
to dispel the fear that accompanies grief.
We cry out to you in our confusion;
comfort us in our affliction.
Help us to travel this road of grief and sadness
with our eyes fixed on the salvation
promised us through the death and resurrection
of your Son,
who is Lord forever and ever.

All: Amen.

Leader: Friends, let us make this place a sign of Christ's peace to the world by sharing that peace with one another.

The prayer service may conclude with an appropriate song.

PRAYER SERVICE FOR PARISH LECTORS

The prayer service may begin with an appropriate song.

CALL TO WORSHIP

Leader:
May the word of God be on our lips.

All:
May the word of God be in our minds and hearts.

OPENING PRAYER

READING OF THE WORD OF GOD

First Reading
Isaiah 55:10–11

Response
R/. See John 6:63c; Psalm 19:7, 8, 9, 10, 11

Leader:
Your words, Lord, are spirit and life.

All:
Your words, Lord, are spirit and life.

Leader:
The law of the LORD is perfect,
   reviving the soul;
the decrees of the LORD are sure,
   making wise the simple.

All:
Your words, Lord, are spirit and life.

Leader:
The precepts of the LORD are right,
   rejoicing the heart;
the commandment of the LORD is clear,
   enlightening the eyes.

All:
Your words, Lord, are spirit and life.

Leader:
The fear of the LORD is pure,
   enduring forever;
the ordinances of the LORD are true
   and righteous altogether.

All:
Your words, Lord, are spirit and life.

Leader:
More to be desired are they than gold,
   even much fine gold;
sweeter also than honey,
   and drippings of the honeycomb.

All:
Your words, Lord, are spirit and life.

Second Reading
1 John 1:1–4

RECOMMITMENT TO THE MINISTRY OF THE WORD

Leader:
Embrace the living word of God.

Lector:
May I be a vessel of the word of life.

At the conclusion of this sign of reverence, all may join in singing a familiar gospel acclamation.

Gospel
Luke 24:44–48

EXTENDED PERIOD OF SILENCE

INTERCESSIONS

LORD'S PRAYER

BLESSING AND DISMISSAL

The prayer service may conclude with an appropriate song.

PRAYER SERVICE FOR MINISTERS OF HOSPITALITY

The prayer service may begin with an appropriate song.

OPENING PRAYER

READING OF THE WORD OF GOD

First Reading
Genesis 18:1–8

Response
Romans 12:9–13

Leader:
May we welcome Christ in one another.

All:
May we welcome Christ in one another.

Leader:
Let love be genuine; hate what is evil, hold fast to what is good.

All:
May we welcome Christ in one another.

Leader:
Love one another with mutual affection; outdo one another in showing honor.

All:
May we welcome Christ in one another.

Leader:
Do not lag in zeal, be ardent in spirit, serve the Lord.

All:
May we welcome Christ in one another.

Leader:
Rejoice in hope, be patient in suffering, persevere in prayer.

All:
May we welcome Christ in one another.

Leader:
Contribute to the needs of the saints; extend hospitality to strangers.

All:
May we welcome Christ in one another.

LORD'S PRAYER

CLOSING PRAYER

BLESSING AND DISMISSAL

The prayer service may conclude with an appropriate song.

Prayer Service for Ministers of Care

The prayer service may begin with an appropriate song.

Opening Prayer

Reading of the Word of God

First Reading
James 5:13–16

Response
Psalm 63

Leader:
O God, you are my God, I seek you,
   my soul thirsts for you;
my flesh faints for you,
   as in a dry and weary land where there is no water.

All:
So I have looked upon you in the sanctuary,
   beholding your power and glory.
Because your steadfast love is better than life,
   my lips will praise you.
So I will bless you as long as I live;
   I will lift up my hands and call on your name.

Leader:
My soul is satisfied as with a rich feast,
   and my mouth praises you with joyful lips
when I think of you on my bed,
   and meditate on you in the watches of the night.

All:
For you have been my help,
   and in the shadow of your wings I sing for joy.
My soul clings to you;
   your right hand upholds me.

Gospel
Matthew 11:28–30

Ritual Anointing

Lord's Prayer

Blessing and Dismissal

The prayer service may conclude with an appropriate song.

PRAYER SERVICE FOR EXTRAORDINARY MINISTERS OF COMMUNION

The prayer service may begin with an appropriate song.

OPENING PRAYER

READING OF THE WORD OF GOD

First Reading
Acts 2:42–47

Response
Psalm 78:3–4, 23–24, 25, 54

Leader:
Things that we have heard and known,
 that our ancestors have told us,
 we will tell to the coming generations
the glorious deeds of the LORD, and his might
 and the wonders that he has done.

All:
Yet he commanded the skies above,
 and opened the doors of heaven;
he rained down on them manna to eat,
 and gave them the grain of heaven.

Leader:
Mortals ate of the bread of angels;
 he sent them food in abundance.

All:
He brought them to his holy hill,
 to the mountain that his right hand had won.

Gospel
Luke 24:13–35

REFLECTIVE SILENCE

BREAKING OF BREAD

LITANY OF PRAISE

LORD'S PRAYER

BLESSING AND DISMISSAL

The prayer service may conclude with an appropriate song.

PRAYER SERVICES FOR PARISH LIFE © 2004, World Library Publications • 800-566-6150 • WLP 017264. Scripture quotations are from the New Revised Standard Version of the Bible © 1989 by the Division of Christian Education of the National Council of the Churches of Christ in the USA. All rights reserved. Used with permission.

PRAYER SERVICE FOR MUSIC MINISTERS

The prayer service may begin with an appropriate song.

OPENING PRAYER

READING OF THE WORD OF GOD

First Reading
2 Chronicles 5:11–14
or
Colossians 3:12–17

Response
Psalm 81:1–2, Isaiah 42:10–11, Psalm 92:1–4,
Psalm 98:1–6

Leader:
Sing aloud to God our strength;
⠀⠀shout for joy to the God of Jacob.

All:
Raise a song, sound the tambourine,
⠀⠀**the sweet lyre with the harp.**
Blow the trumpet at the new moon,
⠀⠀**at the full moon on our festal day.**

Leader:
Sing to the LORD a new song,
⠀⠀his praise from the end of the earth!
Let the sea roar and all that fills it,
⠀⠀the coastlands and their inhabitants.

All:
Let the desert and its towns lift up their voice,
⠀⠀**the villages that Kedar inhabits;**
let the inhabitants of Sela sing for joy,
⠀⠀**let them shout from the tops of the mountains.**

Leader:
It is good to give thanks to the LORD,
⠀⠀to sing praises to your name, O Most High.

All:
To declare your steadfast love in the morning,
⠀⠀**and your faithfulness by night,**
to the music of the lute and the harp,
⠀⠀**to the melody of the lyre.**
For you, O LORD, have made me glad
⠀⠀⠀⠀**by your work;**
⠀⠀**at the works of your hands I sing for joy.**

Leader:
O sing to the LORD a new song,
⠀⠀for he has done marvelous things.
His right hand and his holy arm
⠀⠀have gotten him victory.

All:
The LORD has made known his victory;
⠀⠀**he has revealed his vindication in the sight**
⠀⠀⠀⠀**of the nations.**
He has remembered his steadfast love
⠀⠀⠀⠀**and faithfulness**
⠀⠀**to the house of Israel.**
All the ends of the earth have seen
⠀⠀**the victory of our God.**

Leader:
Make a joyful noise to the LORD, all the earth;
⠀⠀break forth into joyous song and sing praises.

All:
Sing praises to the LORD with the lyre,
⠀⠀**with the lyre and the sound of melody.**
With trumpets and the sound of the horn
⠀⠀**make a joyful noise before the King,**
⠀⠀⠀⠀**the LORD.**

Gospel
Matthew 26:26–30

INTERCESSIONS

Leader:
Sisters and brothers, God calls us to use our
talents to help build the kingdom of God here
on earth. As musicians, we help bring that
kingdom to a reality by creating rhythms and
sounds that give God's people a taste of the life
to come. Let us praise God. O God, you are
the giver of every good gift.

All:
Thank you for the gifts you have so generously
given us.

Leader:
O God, you created the music of nature that
fills the earth.

All:

Help us be attuned to the music of creation that surrounds us.

Leader:

O God, you filled your people, Israel, with a song of praise and thanksgiving.

All:

May their song uphold us in our ministry.

Leader:

O God, you gave voice to the psalmist.

All:

May the singing of psalms continue to inspire us.

Leader:

O God, you sent your Son to be your song of mercy and salvation.

All:

May his song be on our lips and in our hearts.

Leader:

O God, you continue to create music by sending us gifted artists and composers.

All:

Bless their work and lead them closer to your heart.

Leader:

O God, you bless us with voices to sing; with mouths, hands, and feet to play instruments; with ears to hear and to refine our skills.

All:

Bless us, O God, as we make a joyful sound to your name.

LORD'S PRAYER

CLOSING PRAYER

SIGN OF PEACE

The prayer service may conclude with an appropriate song.

PRAYER SERVICES FOR PARISH LIFE © 2004, World Library Publications • 800-566-6150 • WLP 017264. Scripture quotations are from the New Revised Standard Version of the Bible © 1989 by the Division of Christian Education of the National Council of the Churches of Christ in the USA. All rights reserved. Used with permission.

PRAYER SERVICE FOR ALTAR SERVERS

READING OF THE WORD OF GOD

Acts 2:42–47

COMMITMENT TO MINISTRY

Leader:
O God, you call us to serve at your altar.

All:
Give us the help we need to be dedicated servers.

Leader:
O God, you gave us your only Son to be our redeemer.

All:
Strengthen us to be more and more like Christ.

Leader:
O God, you gave us the gift of the Eucharist
as a living reminder of your love for us.

All:
Help us to show awe and reverence for the Eucharist.

Leader:
O God, you are always with us.

All:
Be with us when we are in need.

LORD'S PRAYER

CLOSING PRAYER

BLESSING AND DISMISSAL

SIGN OF PEACE

PRAYER SERVICES FOR PARISH LIFE © 2004, World Library Publications • 800-566-6150 • WLP 017264. All rights reserved.

PRAYER SERVICE FOR A MEETING OF THE LITURGY COMMITTEE

The prayer service may begin with an appropriate song.

OPENING PRAYER

READING OF THE WORD OF GOD

First Reading
Ephesians 4:1–7, 11–13

Response
Psalm 100:1–5

Leader:
Make a joyful noise to the LORD, all the earth.

All:
**Worship the LORD with gladness;
come into his presence with singing.**

Leader:
Know that the LORD is God.

All:
**It is he that made us, and we are his;
we are his people, and the sheep of his pasture.**

Leader:
Enter his gates with thanksgiving,
and his courts with praise.

All:
Give thanks to him, bless his name.

Leader:
For the LORD is good;

All:
**His steadfast love endures forever,
and his faithfulness to all generations.**

Gospel
Matthew 26:17–19

RECOMMITMENT TO MINISTRY

INTERCESSIONS

LORD'S PRAYER

BLESSING AND DISMISSAL

SIGN OF PEACE

The prayer service may conclude with an appropriate song.

Prayer Service for Volunteer Appreciation

The prayer service may begin with an appropriate song.

Opening Prayer

Reading of the Word of God

First Reading
Philippians 4:4–9

Response
Psalm 112:1–9

Leader:
Praise the LORD!
   Happy are those who fear the LORD,
    who greatly delight in his commandments.
Their descendants will be mighty in the land;
   the generation of the upright will be blessed.

All:
**Wealth and riches are in their houses,
   and their righteousness endures forever.
They rise in the darkness as a light
    for the upright;
   they are gracious, merciful, and righteous.**

Leader:
It is well with those who deal generously and lend,
   who conduct their affairs with justice.
For the righteous will never be moved;
   they will be remembered forever.

All:
**They are not afraid of evil tidings;
   their hearts are firm, secure in the LORD.
Their hearts are steady;
    they will not be afraid;
   in the end they will look in triumph
    on their foes.
They have distributed freely, they have given
    to the poor;
   their righteousness endures forever.**

Gospel
Matthew 5:13–16

Recommitment to Parish Ministry and Service

Sharing the Light of Christ

Leader:
Sisters and brothers, are you willing to share the light of Christ with others?

All:
We are.

Leader:
Do you promise never to hide your light,
but always keep it burning in service to God's people?

All:
We do.

Leader:
Are you willing to respond with love to those who seek the living God?

All:
We are.

Leader:
Friends, we praise and thank God for the great gifts planted in each one of us at the moment of our baptism. We ask God to continue to nurture us on our journeys of faith and to help us keep the flame of faith bravely burning. In thanksgiving to God, let us all join in praying Psalm 138.

All:
**I give you thanks, O LORD,
    with my whole heart.
I bow down toward your holy temple
   and give thanks to your name
    for your steadfast love
    and your faithfulness;
   for you have exalted your name
    and your word
   above everything.
On the day I called you answered me,
   you increased my strength of soul.
All the kings of the earth shall praise you,
    O LORD,
   for they have heard the words
    of your mouth.
They shall sing the ways of the LORD,
   for great is the glory of the LORD.**

Psalm 138:1a, 2–5

Closing Prayer

Blessing

Leader:
May God bless us, ✠
protect us from evil,
and bring us to everlasting life.

All:
May God strengthen us in faith,
keep us in hope,
and shower us with love. Amen.

The prayer service may conclude with an appropriate song.

PRAYER SERVICE TO WELCOME NEW PARISHIONERS

OPENING PRAYER

READING OF THE WORD OF GOD

Romans 12:3–5, 12–13

Response
Psalm 100:1–5

All:

Make a joyful noise to the LORD, all the earth.
Worship the LORD with gladness;
   come into his presence with singing.

Know that the LORD is God.
   It is he that made us, and we are his;
   we are his people, and the sheep of his pasture.

Enter his gates with thanksgiving,
   and his courts with praise.
   Give thanks to him, bless his name.

For the LORD is good;
   his steadfast love endures forever,
   and his faithfulness to all generations.

LORD'S PRAYER

CLOSING PRAYER

SIGN OF PEACE

PRAYER FOR A PARISH MEETING

AT THE BEGINNING OF THE MEETING

Leader:
Let us pray for God's help
and the inspiration of the Holy Spirit
during our meeting.

READING OF THE WORD OF GOD

2 Corinthians 4:13–15

Response
Job 33:3–4

All:
My words declare the uprightness of my heart
    and what my lips know they speak sincerely.
The spirit of God has made me,
    and the breath of the Almighty gives me life.

INTERCESSIONS

•

AT THE CLOSE OF THE MEETING

READING OF THE WORD OF GOD

Ephesians 3:14–19

Response
Ephesians 3:20–21

All:
Now to him who by the power at work within us
is able to accomplish abundantly
far more than all we can ask or imagine,
to him be glory in the church
and in Christ Jesus to all generations
forever and ever. Amen.

Parish Picnic

The prayer service may begin with an appropriate song.

Call to Celebration

Leader:
God looked at everything that had been made.

All:
And found it very good.

Opening Prayer

Reading of the Word of God

Matthew 6:26–33

Blessing of Food

Leader:
Our help comes from the LORD.

All:
Who made heaven and earth.

Psalm 121:2

Prayer

Concluding Rite

At the close of the picnic, all gather in thanksgiving.

Leader:
Please respond "We thank you, Lord" after each invocation.

For this time to enjoy the earth,
one another, and you, O Lord:
R/. We thank you, Lord.

For the beautiful sight of sunshine and flowers,
grass and trees, butterflies, and gliding birds: **R/.**

For the delightful sounds of calling birds,
rushing water, and crackling campfires: **R/.**

For the enjoyable scents of fresh air,
roasting hot dogs, and steaming coffee: **R/.**

For the pleasant touch of grass and sand,
the warmth of the sun,
the stimulation of the wind and water: **R/.**

For this time to re-create ourselves
in body, mind, and spirit: **R/.**

For the refreshment of exercise,
the calm away from the pressures of work: **R/.**

For this relaxed time to renew the bonds of love
sometimes overlooked in the routine of daily
work: **R/.**

For all who try to make this earth a better place
to live: **R/.**

Departure

Leader:
Let us return home refreshed in body and spirit.

All:
Thanks be to God.

The prayer service may conclude with an appropriate song.

PRAYER BEFORE A PARISH TRIP

The prayer service may begin with an appropriate song.

CALL TO WORSHIP

Leader:
May we be blessed in the city,
    and blessed in the country!

All:
**May we be blessed in our coming in,
    and blessed in our going out!**

OPENING PRAYER

READING OF THE WORD OF GOD

Joshua 24:17, 18b

Response
Psalm 121:5, 8

All:
**The LORD is our keeper;
    the LORD is our shade at our right hand.
The LORD will keep our going out
      and our coming in
from this time on and forevermore.**

PRAYER

Leader:
O God, you have given your angels charge
over us,

All:
To guard us in all our undertakings.

Leader:
Let us pray.
O God, we marvel at your providence,
which has given your holy angels care over us.
You protected your people, Israel, on their
sojourn in the desert. Watch over us
in our travels.

Liten to our prayers for your blessing,
that we may be safe under your protection
and happy in your company through all eternity.
We ask this through Christ our Lord.

All:
Amen.

CONCLUDING RITE

Leader:
May the almighty and merciful Lord
lead us along ways of peace and contentment,
and may the angel Raphael accompany us on
our journey,

All:
**So we may return to our home
in peace, health, and joy.**

The prayer service may conclude with an appropriate song.

CELEBRATING THE GIFT OF GOD'S CREATION

We celebrate our blessings and pray that all people may protect these gifts from needless, selfish destruction. This service may be celebrated outdoors in a place of natural beauty.

The prayer service may begin with an appropriate song.

CALL TO CELEBRATION

Leader:
Open your eyes, your hearts, your whole selves, and sense the good things we have from the Lord our God.

All:
Blessed be our God forever.

OPENING PRAYER

READING OF THE WORD OF GOD

Deuteronomy 8:7–14

LITANY OF PRAISE AND THANKSGIVING

(In the style of Daniel 3:52–90)

Leader:
Blest are you, O Lord, the God of creation.
All:
Praiseworthy and exalted forever.

Leader:
Blest are you, Lord of the nations.
All:
Praiseworthy and exalted forever.

Leader:
Bless the Lord, all you works of the Lord.
All:
Praise and exalt God forever.

Leader:
Northern lights and sunny days, bless the Lord.
All:
Praise and exalt God forever.

Leader:
Twinkling stars and darkest night, bless the Lord.
All:
Praise and exalt God forever.

Leader:
Sky and clouds and heaven above, bless the Lord.
All:
Praise and exalt God forever.

Leader:
Dew and fog and glistening frost, bless the Lord.
All:
Praise and exalt God forever.

Leader:
All you winds, bless the Lord.
All:
Praise and exalt God forever.

Leader:
All you seasons, bless the Lord.
All:
Praise and exalt God forever.

Leader:
Tundra and deserts, fields and plains, bless the Lord.
All:
Praise and exalt God forever.

Leader:
All mountains and hills, bless the Lord.
All:
Praise and exalt God forever.

Leader:
All lakes and ponds, bless the Lord.
All:
Praise and exalt God forever.

Leader:
All rivers and streams, bless the Lord.
All:
Praise and exalt God forever.

Leader:
Hot springs, geysers, and fountains, bless the Lord.
All:
Praise and exalt God forever.

Leader:
Coal mines, gold and silver mines, gravel pits, and oil wells, bless the Lord.
All:
Praise and exalt God forever.

Leader:
All you animals wild and tame, bless the Lord.
All:
Praise and exalt God forever.

Leader:
All you birds of the air, bless the Lord.
All:
Praise and exalt God forever.

Leader:
All you fish in the shallows and depths, bless the Lord.
All:
Praise and exalt God forever.

Leader:
All you natural resources and wealth of this land, bless the Lord.
All:
Praise and exalt God forever.

Leader:
All you commerce and industry, business and trade, bless the Lord.
All:
Praise and exalt God forever.

Leader:
Church bells, school bells, and cow bells, bless the Lord.
All:
Praise and exalt God forever.

Leader:
Cities and towns, suburbs, farms, and ranches, bless the Lord.
All:
Praise and exalt God forever.

Leader:
Automobiles and trains, airplanes and ships, bless the Lord.
All:
Praise and exalt God forever.

Leader:
Bicycles, scooters, wagons, and all moving things, bless the Lord.
All:
Praise and exalt God forever.

Leader:
Train whistles, factory whistles, and all whistles, bless the Lord.
All:
Praise and exalt God forever.

Leader:
Skyscrapers and hotels, hogans and teepees, bungalows and apartments, bless the Lord.
All:
Praise and exalt God forever.

Leader:
Citizens of this land, bless the Lord.
All:
Praise and exalt God forever.

A talk or discussion may follow this litany. Participants could prepare slides or other presentations. These activities may initiate and stimulate local ecological programs.

CONCLUDING RITE

Leader:
Filled with God's praises,
we return home glorifying the Lord.
May peace be with us all, now and forever.

All:
Amen.

The prayer service may conclude with an appropriate song.

ADVENT PENITENTIAL SERVICE

The prayer service may begin with an appropriate song.

CALL TO WORSHIP

Leader:
Seek the LORD while he may be found,
   call upon him while he is near.

Isaiah 55:6

All:
**Let us turn our hearts to the LORD,
   whose mercy knows no end.**

Leader:
Lord Jesus, you were foretold by the prophets:
Lord, have mercy.

All:
Lord, have mercy.

Leader:
Lord Jesus, you came to save us from sin:
Christ, have mercy.

All:
Christ, have mercy.

Leader:
Lord Jesus, you are the Light who scatters the
darkness of sin:
Lord, have mercy.

All:
Lord, have mercy.

OPENING PRAYER

READING OF THE WORD OF GOD

First Reading
1 John 1:5 — 2:2

Response
Psalm 25:8-11

All:
**Good and upright is the LORD;
   therefore he instructs sinners in the way.
He leads the humble in what is right,
   and teaches the humble his way.
All the paths of the LORD are steadfast love
      and faithfulness,**

**for those who keep his covenant
   and his decrees.
For your name's sake, O LORD,
   pardon my guilt, for it is great.**

Gospel
John 3:16–21

EXAMINATION OF CONSCIENCE

All:
**I confess to Almighty God,
and to you, my brothers and sisters,
that I have sinned through my own fault**
(All strike their breast.)
**in my thoughts and in my words,
in what I have done,
and in what I have failed to do;
and I ask blessed Mary, ever virgin,
all the angels and saints,
and you, my brothers and sisters,
to pray for me to the Lord our God.**

Psalm 51:1–17

Leader:
Have mercy on me, O God,
   according to your steadfast love;
according to your abundant mercy
   blot out my transgressions.
Wash me thoroughly from my iniquity,
   and cleanse me from my sin.

All:
**For I know my transgressions,
   and my sin is ever before me.
Against you, you alone, have I sinned,
   and done what is evil in your sight,
so that you are justified in your sentence
   and blameless when you pass judgment.**

Leader:
Indeed, I was born guilty,
   a sinner when my mother conceived me.
You desire truth in the inward being;
   therefore teach me wisdom in
      my secret heart.

All:
Purge me with hyssop, and I shall be clean;
  wash me, and I shall be whiter than snow.
Let me hear joy and gladness;
  let the bones that you have crushed rejoice.
Hide your face from my sins,
  and blot out all my iniquities.

Leader:
Create in me a clean heart, O God,
  and put a new and right spirit within me.
Do not cast me away from your presence,
  and do not take your holy spirit from me.
Restore to me the joy of your salvation,
  and sustain in me a willing spirit.

All:
Then I will teach transgressors your ways,
  and sinners will return to you.
Deliver me from bloodshed, O God,
  O God of my salvation,
  and my tongue will sing aloud
    of your deliverance.

Leader:
O Lord, open my lips,
  and my mouth will declare your praise.
For you have no delight in sacrifice;
  if I were to give a burnt offering, you would
    not be pleased.

All:
The sacrifice acceptable to God
    is a broken spirit;
  a broken and contrite heart, O God,
    you will not despise.

LORD'S PRAYER

[INDIVIDUAL CONFESSION AND ABSOLUTION]

PROCLAMATION OF PRAISE FOR GOD'S MERCY
Luke 1:46–55

All:
My soul magnifies the Lord,
  and my spirit rejoices in God my Savior,
for he has looked with favor on the lowliness
      of his servant.
    Surely, from now on all generations
      will call me blessed;
for the Mighty One has done great things for me,
  and holy is his name.
His mercy is for those who fear him
  from generation to generation.
He has shown strength with his arm;
  he has scattered the proud in the thoughts
      of their hearts.
He has brought down the powerful
      from their thrones,
  and lifted up the lowly;
he has filled the hungry with good things,
  and sent the rich away empty.
He has helped his servant Israel,
  in remembrance of his mercy,
according to the promise he made
      to our ancestors,
  to Abraham and to his descendants forever.

CLOSING PRAYER

DISMISSAL

Leader:
Go in peace,
and may Jesus the Light shine on your path
and in your heart forever.

All:
Thanks be to God.

The prayer service may conclude with an appropriate song.

LENTEN PENITENTIAL SERVICE

The prayer service may begin with an appropriate song.

CALL TO WORSHIP

Lamentations 3:40–41

Leader:
Let us test and examine our ways,
   and return to the Lord.

All:
Let us lift up our hearts as well as our hands
   to God in heaven.

OPENING PRAYER

READING OF THE WORD OF GOD

First Reading
Hosea 14:1–3, 9

Response
Psalm 119:89, 28, 105

Leader:
The LORD exists forever;
   your word is firmly fixed in heaven.

All:
My soul melts away for sorrow;
   strengthen me according to your word.

Leader:
Your word is a lamp to my feet
   and a light to my path.

Gospel
John 20:19–23

EXAMINATION OF CONSCIENCE

All:
I confess to Almighty God,
and to you, my brothers and sisters,
that I have sinned through my own fault
(All strike their breast.)
in my thoughts and in my words,
in what I have done,
and in what I have failed to do;

and I ask blessed Mary, ever virgin,
all the angels and saints,
and you, my brothers and sisters,
to pray for me to the Lord our God.

LITANY

Leader:
At an acceptable time I have listened to you,
   and on a day of salvation I have helped you.
2 Corinthians 6:2

All:
The kindness of God leads us to repentance.

Leader:
Come now, let us argue it out,
   says the LORD:
though your sins are like scarlet,
   they shall be like snow;
though they are red like crimson,
   they shall become like wool.
Isaiah 1:18

All:
Cleanse me from my sin.
Wash me, and I shall be whiter than snow.
Psalm 51:2, 7b

Leader:
Come, let us walk in the light of the Lord!

All:
The night is far gone, the day is near.
Let us then lay aside the works of darkness
and put on the armor of light.
Romans 13:12

RESOLUTION

Leader:
Our God acts not out of whimsy but by careful
design. Thus all the important acts of salvation
have followed a period of purification and
preparation.

All:
For everything there is a season,
and a time for every matter under heaven.
Ecclesiastes 3:1

Leader:

Before the covenant with the human race was made with Noah, a period of rain separated the just from the unjust.

All:

The rain fell on the earth forty days and forty nights.

Genesis 7:12

Leader:

Before the covenant was given on Mount Sinai, Moses underwent a period of preparation.

All:

Moses entered the cloud, and went up on the mountain. Moses was on the mountain for forty days and forty nights.

Exodus 24:18

Leader:

Before the prophet Elijah could commune with God, he had to undergo a period of pilgrimage.

All:

**Elijah got up, and ate and drank;
then he went in the strength of that food
forty days and forty nights to Horeb
   the mount of God.**

1 Kings 19:8

Leader:

Before the beginning of his public ministry, Jesus experienced a period of testing in the desert.

All:

Jesus, full of the Holy Spirit, returned from the Jordan and was led by the Spirit in the wilderness, where for forty days he was tempted by the devil.

Luke 4:1–2

Leader:

Before his return to the Father, the risen Lord prepared the disciples for the church's mission.

All:

After his suffering he presented himself alive to them by many convincing proofs, appearing to them during forty days and speaking about the kingdom of God.

Acts 1:3

Leader:

Now we are gathered to celebrate another period of forty days, a period of preparation whose goal is the glory of Easter.

All:

Therefore, since we are surrounded by so great a cloud of witnesses, let us also lay aside every weight and the sin that clings so closely, and let us run with perseverance the race that is set before us, looking to Jesus the pioneer and perfecter of our faith, who for the sake of the joy that was set before him endured the cross, disregarding its shame, and has taken his seat at the right hand of the throne of God.

Hebrews 12:1–2

LORD'S PRAYER

[INDIVIDUAL CONFESSION AND ABSOLUTION]

PROCLAMATION OF PRAISE FOR GOD'S MERCY

Ephesians 1:3–8a

All:

Blessed be the God and Father of
our Lord Jesus Christ,
who has blessed us in Christ
with every spiritual blessing
in the heavenly places,
just as he chose us in Christ
before the foundation of the world
to be holy and blameless before him in love.
He destined us for adoption as his children
through Jesus Christ,
according to the good pleasure of his will,
to the praise of his glorious grace
that he freely bestowed on us in the Beloved.
In him we have redemption
through his blood,
the forgiveness of our trespasses,
according to the riches of his grace
that he lavished on us.

CLOSING PRAYER

DISMISSAL

Leader:

Having been renewed in heart and mind,
go in the peace of Christ.

All:

Thanks be to God.

The prayer service may conclude with an appropriate song.

PENITENTIAL SERVICE: HOPE

The prayer service may begin with an appropriate song.

CALL TO WORSHIP
Psalm 62:7–8

Leader:
On God rests my deliverance and my honor;
  my mighty rock, my refuge is in God.

All:
Trust in him at all times, O people;
  pour out your hearts before him;
God is a refuge for us.

OPENING PRAYER

READING OF THE WORD OF GOD

First Reading
Job 11:13–18

Gospel
John 14:1–3, 18–19

EXAMINATION OF CONSCIENCE

All:
I confess to Almighty God,
and to you, my brothers and sisters,
that I have sinned through my own fault
(All strike their breast.)
in my thoughts and in my words,
in what I have done,
and in what I have failed to do;
and I ask blessed Mary, ever virgin,
all the angels and saints,
and you, my brothers and sisters,
to pray for me to the Lord our God.

LITANY

Leader:
Let us rejoice in hope;
let us be patient under trial;
let us persevere in prayer.

Reader:
As we strive to admonish the sinner,
and as we are aware of our sins:

All:
R/. We trust in your help, O Lord.

Reader:
As we attempt to instruct the ignorant,
and as we admit our own ignorance of the ways
of God: **R/.**

As we try to counsel the doubtful,
and as we attempt to live with our doubts: **R/.**

As we seek to comfort the sorrowful,
and as we succumb to self-pity: **R/.**

As we strive to bear wrongs patiently,
and as we find it hard to forgive all injuries: **R/.**

As we are mindful of the living and the dead,
and as we pray for their eternal happiness: **R/.**

LORD'S PRAYER

[INDIVIDUAL CONFESSION AND ABSOLUTION]

PROCLAMATION OF PRAISE FOR GOD'S MERCY
Acts 2:25–28

All:
I saw the Lord always before me, for he is at my
right hand so that I will not be shaken; there-
fore my heart was glad, and my tongue rejoiced;
moreover my flesh will live in hope. For you will
not abandon my soul to Hades, or let your Holy
One experience corruption. You have made
known to me the ways of life; you will make me
full of gladness with your presence.

CLOSING PRAYER

DISMISSAL

Leader:
Living in joyful hope for the coming of the Lord,
we go forth in the peace of Christ.

All:
Thanks be to God.

The prayer service may conclude with an appropriate song.

PRAYER SERVICES FOR PARISH LIFE © 2004, World Library Publications • 800-566-6150 • WLP 017264. Scripture quotations are from the New Revised Standard Version
of the Bible © 1989 by the Division of Christian Education of the National Council of the Churches of Christ in the USA. The English translation of the *Confiteor*
from *The Roman Missal* © 1973, International Committee on English in the Liturgy, Inc. All rights reserved. Used with permission.

PENITENTIAL SERVICE: A NEW BEGINNING

With special New Year rites, ancient peoples endeavored to abolish the past so that there could be a new birth of times. After rites of purification, confession of sin, and exorcism, the people entered another cycle of time. They were refreshed and reborn in spirit. In our time, New Year's resolutions reflect these efforts to make things new. This is a new year. Before much of it slips into the past, we take time to consider this new beginning. The prayer service may begin with an appropriate song.

CALL TO A NEW BEGINNING
Ephesians 5:8–9

Leader:
Once we were darkness.

All:
Now in the Lord we are light.

Leader:
The fruit of the light is found in all that is good and right and true.

All:
Let us live as children of the light.

OPENING PRAYER

READING OF THE WORD OF GOD

First Reading
Hosea 6:1–3

RESPONSE

Leader:
Creative love of the Father,
All:
Renew the face of the earth.

Leader:
Jesus among us,
All:
Renew the face of the earth.

Leader:
Continuing guidance of the Holy Spirit,
All:
Renew the face of the earth.

Leader:
Caring for one another,
All:
We are people of light.

Leader:
With sacrifices throughout the year,
All:
We are people of light.

Leader:
Giving food to the hungry and drink to the thirsty,
All:
We are people of light.

Leader:
Clothing the naked and sheltering the homeless,
All:
We are people of light.

Leader:
Visiting the imprisoned and the sick,
All:
We are people of light.

Leader:
Burying the dead,
All:
We are people of light.

Leader:
Shedding our selfishness and sin,
All:
We are people of light.

Leader:
Forgiving one another,
All:
We are people of light.

Gospel
Luke 13:6–9

REFLECTION
Pause for reflection after each thought. The leader may also offer a brief reflection based on these ideas.

The signs of life I give to others are . . .

My tree of life bears fruit when . . .

Jesus' light shines through me when . . .

For the New Year I will try . . .

EXAMINATION OF CONSCIENCE

All:

I confess to Almighty God,
and to you, my brothers and sisters,
that I have sinned through my own fault
(All strike their breast.)
in my thoughts and in my words,
in what I have done,
and in what I have failed to do;
and I ask blessed Mary, ever virgin,
all the angels and saints,
and you, my brothers and sisters,
to pray for me to the Lord our God.

LORD'S PRAYER

[INDIVIDUAL CONFESSION AND ABSOLUTION]

PROCLAMATION OF PRAISE FOR GOD'S MERCY

Isaiah 12:1–2, 4b–6

All:

I will give thanks to you, O LORD,
   for though you were angry with me,
your anger turned away,
   and you comforted me.
Surely God is my salvation;
   I will trust, and will not be afraid,
for the LORD GOD is my strength and my might;
   he has become my salvation.
Give thanks to the LORD,
   call on his name;
make known his deeds among the nations;
   proclaim that his name is exalted.
Sing praise to the LORD,
     for he has done gloriously;
   let this be known in all the earth.
Shout aloud and sing for joy, O royal Zion,
   for great in your midst is the Holy One
     of Israel.

CLOSING PRAYER

DISMISSAL

Leader:
May the almighty Lord order our days and
deeds in peace, and lead us to everlasting light.

All:
Amen.

The prayer service may conclude with an appropriate song.

PRAYER SERVICES FOR PARISH LIFE © 2004, World Library Publications • 800-566-6150 • WLP 017264. Scripture quotations are from the New Revised Standard Version of the Bible © 1989 by the Division of Christian Education of the National Council of the Churches of Christ in the USA. The English translation of the *Confiteor* from *The Roman Missal* © 1973, International Committee on English in the Liturgy, Inc. All rights reserved. Used with permission.

PENITENTIAL SERVICE: RESPECT FOR LIFE

The prayer service may begin with an appropriate song.

CALL TO WORSHIP

Leader:
Blessed be the God and Father of our Lord Jesus Christ! By his great mercy he has given us a new birth into a living hope through the resurrection of Jesus Christ from the dead.

1 Peter 1:3

All:
In him we live and move and have our being.

Acts 17:28

OPENING PRAYER

READING OF THE WORD OF GOD

First Reading
Deuteronomy 30:15–20a

Response
Psalm 27:1, 13

All:
The LORD is my light and my salvation;
   whom shall I fear?
The LORD is the stronghold of my life,
   of whom shall I be afraid?
I believe that I shall see the goodness
      of the LORD
   in the land of the living.

Gospel
Matthew 25:31–40

INTERCESSIONS

EXAMINATION OF CONSCIENCE

All:
I confess to Almighty God,
and to you, my brothers and sisters,
that I have sinned through my own fault
(All strike their breast.)
in my thoughts and in my words,
in what I have done,
and in what I have failed to do;
and I ask blessed Mary, ever virgin,
all the angels and saints,
and you, my brothers and sisters,
to pray for me to the Lord our God.

LORD'S PRAYER

[INDIVIDUAL CONFESSION AND ABSOLUTION]

CLOSING PRAYER

BLESSING

The prayer service may conclude with an appropriate song.

MEAL BLESSING: ADVENT

O God our creator,
we ask for your blessing on the food
and the friendships we share.
As we wait in joyful hope
for the coming of your Son,
keep us mindful of those who have nothing to eat.
Inspire us to work to bring food to the hungry,
shelter to the homeless,
and hope to those who despair.
Bless those who have prepared this meal,
and bless us as we enjoy the abundance
of your gifts of food and drink.
We ask this through Christ our Lord. Amen.

PRAYER SERVICES FOR PARISH LIFE © 2004, World Library Publications • 800-566-6150 • WLP 017264. All rights reserved.

Meal Blessing: Christmas Season

O God of wonder,
you sent your Son, Jesus,
as a blessing upon all who dwell upon the earth.
Send your blessing upon the food we are about to share,
on those who provided it for us,
and upon those who prepared it.
As we enjoy this meal,
keep us mindful of those who have nothing to eat.
May the sharing of this meal
renew our efforts to bring the good news to the poor.
We ask this through Christ our Lord. Amen.

Prayer Services for Parish Life © 2004, World Library Publications • 800-566-6150 • WLP 017264. All rights reserved.

MEAL BLESSING: LENT

O God of mercy and compassion,
with humility of heart
we ask your blessing on the meal we are about to share.
During this season of prayer, fasting, and almsgiving
may we be inspired to share our gifts with the needy.
May the sharing of this meal
urge us on to work tirelessly to bring your word of comfort
to all who seek meaning and direction in their lives.
Bless us, the food we are about to receive,
those who prepared it,
and the friendships we share.
We ask this in the name of your Son, Jesus Christ,
who is Lord forever and ever. Amen.

MEAL BLESSING
LENTEN SIMPLE MEAL

Merciful God,
we gather in this place to share a simple meal.
Let this meal remind us that
hundreds of millions of people across this planet
will go to sleep hungry this very night.
May our Lenten sacrifice
help those who are in need
in this community and beyond.
Bless this food,
those who have prepared this meal,
and those who will clean up when it is finished.
As we continue our Lenten journey,
keep our eyes fixed on the upcoming celebration
of the passion, death, and resurrection of your Son,
who is Lord forever and ever. Amen.

PRAYER SERVICES FOR PARISH LIFE © 2004, World Library Publications • 800-566-6150 • WLP 017264. All rights reserved.

Meal Blessing: Easter Season

You shower us with blessings,
O God of love.
In this season of joy,
when we celebrate Christ's death and resurrection,
you continue to bless and protect us.
As we prepare to share this meal,
keep us mindful of those who this night will die of hunger.
As believers who have put on Christ in baptism,
make us bearers of gospel justice.
Bless this food and the friendships we share.
We ask this through Christ our Lord. Amen.

MEAL BLESSING: ORDINARY TIME

You give us every good gift,
O God of the covenant.
Help us to see in the food spread before us
another outpouring of your grace.
Be with us as we share this meal
and keep us ever mindful of the hungry.
Bless us and the food we are about to receive.
We ask this through Christ our Lord. Amen.

PRAYER SERVICES FOR PARISH LIFE © 2004, World Library Publications • 800-566-6150 • WLP 017264. All rights reserved.

PRAYER SERVICE FOR BAPTISM PREPARATION SESSIONS

The prayer service may begin with an appropriate song.

READING OF THE WORD OF GOD

First Reading
1 Peter 2:4–5, 9–10

Response
Psalm 23:1– 6

Leader:
The LORD is my shepherd, I shall not want.
    He makes me lie down in green pastures;
he leads me beside still waters;
    he restores my soul.

All:
The LORD is my shepherd, I shall not want.
    He makes me lie down in green pastures;
he leads me beside still waters;
    he restores my soul.

Leader:
He leads me in right paths
    for his name's sake.
Even though I walk through the darkest valley,
    I fear no evil;

All:
For you are with me;
    your rod and your staff—
    they comfort me.

Leader:
You prepare a table before me
    in the presence of my enemies;

All:
You anoint my head with oil;
    my cup overflows.

Leader:
Surely goodness and mercy shall follow me
    all the days of my life;

All:
And I shall dwell in the house of the Lord
    my whole life long.

Leader:
The LORD is my shepherd, I shall not want.
    He makes me lie down in green pastures;
he leads me beside still waters;
    he restores my soul.

All:
The LORD is my shepherd, I shall not want.
    He makes me lie down in green pastures;
he leads me beside still waters;
    he restores my soul.

Gospel
Mark 10:13–16

BAPTISMAL RECOMMITMENT

INTERCESSIONS

LORD'S PRAYER

CLOSING PRAYER

SIGN OF PEACE

The prayer service may conclude with an appropriate song.

PRAYER SERVICE FOR ENGAGED COUPLES PREPARING FOR MARRIAGE

The prayer service may begin with an appropriate song.

CALL TO WORSHIP

Leader:
Sisters and brothers, God has drawn you into each other's lives and given you the grace of love and companionship. We praise God for these gifts and ask God to nurture them. As you prepare to celebrate your wedding, look to God to be your strength and your guide. Let us lift our hearts and voices in prayer.

All:
God of everlasting love and truth,
thank you for a gift that is beyond measure:
the gift of the one with whom I will share
the rest of my life.
Strengthen us as our relationship unfolds.
Do not let us forget that it is you who have
drawn us together.
Help us always to recognize your presence
in our marriage
and keep us always under your care
and protection.
We ask this through Christ our Lord. Amen.

READING OF THE WORD OF GOD

First Reading
Colossians 3:12–17

Response
Psalm 103:1–2, 8, 13, 17–18a

Leader:
Bless the LORD, O my soul,
  and all that is within me,
  bless his holy name.

All:
Bless the LORD, O my soul,
  and all that is within me
  bless his holy name.

Leader:
Bless the LORD, O my soul,
  and do not forget all his benefits.

All:
The LORD is merciful and gracious,
  slow to anger and abounding
  in steadfast love.

Leader:
As a father has compassion for his children,
  so the LORD has compassion for those
  who fear him.

All:
But the steadfast love of the LORD is from
  everlasting to everlasting
  on those who fear him,
  and his righteousness to children's children,
to those who keep his covenants
  and remember to do his commandments.

Leader:
Bless the LORD, O my soul,
  and all that is within me,
  bless his holy name.

All:
Bless the LORD, O my soul,
  and all that is within me,
  bless his holy name.

Gospel
John 15:9–12

PLEDGE OF COMMITMENT TO GOD'S WORD

LORD'S PRAYER

CLOSING PRAYER

SIGN OF PEACE

The prayer service may conclude with an appropriate song.

PRAYER SERVICES FOR PARISH LIFE © 2004, **World Library Publications** • 800-566-6150 • WLP 017264. Scripture quotations are from the New Revised Standard Version of the Bible © 1989 by the Division of Christian Education of the National Council of the Churches of Christ in the USA. All rights reserved. Used with permission.

PRAYER SERVICE FOR CHRISTIAN UNITY

The prayer service may begin with an appropriate song.

CALL TO PRAYER

Leader:
Come, let us return to the LORD; . . .
 he will heal us . . .
 and he will bind us up.

Hosea 6:1

All:
**Let us look to him, and be radiant;
 that our faces shall never be ashamed.**

Psalm 34:5

Leader:
Let us express our faith as we pray the words
handed down to us through Christian tradition
as the Apostles' Creed.

All:
**I believe in God, the Father almighty,
 creator of heaven and earth.
I believe in Jesus Christ, his only Son,
  our Lord.
 He was conceived by the power
  of the Holy Spirit
  and born of the Virgin Mary.
 He suffered under Pontius Pilate,
  was crucified, died, and was buried.
 He descended to the dead.
 On the third day he rose again.
 He ascended into heaven,
  and is seated at the right hand
   of the Father.
 He will come again to judge the living
  and the dead.
I believe in the Holy Spirit,
 the holy catholic Church,
 the communion of saints,
 the forgiveness of sins,
 the resurrection of the body,
 and life everlasting. Amen.**

READING OF THE WORD OF GOD

First Reading
Leviticus 26:3–4, 9, 12

Response
Jeremiah 31:10, 11–12ab, 13–14

Leader:
R/. Lord, gather your scattered people.

All:
R/. Lord, gather your scattered people.

Leader:
Hear the word of the LORD, O nations,
 and declare it in the coastlands far away;
say, "He who scattered Israel will gather him,
 and will keep him
  as a shepherd a flock." **R/.**

Leader:
For the LORD has ransomed Jacob,
 and has redeemed him from hands
  too strong for him.
They shall come and sing aloud
  on the height of Zion,
 and they shall be radiant over the goodness
  of the LORD. **R/.**

Leader:
Then shall the young women rejoice
  in the dance,
 and the young men and the old
  shall be merry.
I will turn their mourning into joy,
 I will comfort them and give them
  gladness for sorrow. **R/.**

Second Reading
Ephesians 2:19–22

Gospel
John 10:11–16

INTERCESSIONS

(Based on Ephesians 4:5–6, 31–32)

Leader:
Hope for Christian unity begins with respect
for one another. Let us pray for peace and
harmony among all people.

All:
**Father, may those divided by anger, fear, or
misunderstanding see the truth and forgive
one another.**

Leader:
Let us pray for Christian unity.

All:
May we see the blessings of variety in our traditions and find unity in one Lord, one faith, one baptism, one God and Father.

We may add other intentions, with the response: **Lord, hear our prayer.**

LORD'S PRAYER

BLESSING

Leader:
May the God of steadfastness and encourgement
grant you to live in harmony with one another,
in accordance with Christ Jesus,
so that you may with one voice
glorify the God and Father of our Lord Jesus Christ.

All:
Amen.

The prayer service may conclude with an appropriate song.

PRAYER SERVICES FOR PARISH LIFE © 2004, World Library Publications • 800-566-6150 • WLP 017264. Scripture quotations are from the New Revised Standard Version of the Bible © 1989 by the Division of Christian Education of the National Council of the Churches of Christ in the USA. All rights reserved. Used with permission.

A Lenten Service Based on the Final Words of Christ

The prayer service may begin with an appropriate song.

Call to Celebration

Leader:
Draw near to God, and he will draw near to you.

James 4:8

All:
Hear my cry, O God;
listen to my prayer.

Psalm 61:1

Opening Prayer

Reading of the Word of God

I

Luke 23:32–34
Two others also, who were criminals, were led away to be put to death with Jesus. When they came to the place that is called The Skull, they crucified Jesus there with the criminals, one on his right and one on his left. Then Jesus said,

All:
"Father, forgive them; for they do not know what they are doing."

Silent prayer, reflective music, or meditative comment may follow.

Leader:
Have mercy on us, O Lord.

All:
Jesus, we believe in you, we hope in you, we love you. Through your cross you brought us the hope of resurrection.

II

Luke 23:39–43
One of the criminals who were hanged there kept deriding him and saying, "Are you not the Messiah? Save yourself and us!" But the other rebuked him, saying, "Do you not fear God, since you are under the same sentence of condemnation? And we indeed have been condemned justly, for we are getting what we deserve for our deeds, but this man has done nothing wrong." Then he said, "Jesus, remember me when you come into your kingdom." He replied,

All:
"Truly I tell you, today you will be with me in Paradise."

Silent prayer, reflective music, or meditative comment may follow.

Leader:
Have mercy on us, O Lord.

All:
Jesus, we believe in you, we hope in you, we love you. Through your cross you brought us the hope of resurrection.

III

John 19:25–27
Standing near the cross of Jesus were his mother, and his mother's sister, Mary the wife of Clopas, and Mary Magdalene. When Jesus saw his mother and the disciple whom he loved standing beside her, he said to his mother,

All:
"Woman, here is your son."

Leader:
Then he said to the disciple,

All:
"Here is your mother."

Silent prayer, reflective music, or meditative comment may follow.

Leader:
Have mercy on us, O Lord.

All:
Jesus, we believe in you, we hope in you, we love you. Through your cross you brought us the hope of resurrection.

IV

Matthew 27:45–46

From noon on, darkness came over the whole land until three in the afternoon. And about three o'clock Jesus cried with a loud voice,

All:

"My God, my God, why have you forsaken me?"

Silent prayer, reflective music, or meditative comment may follow.

Leader:

Have mercy on us, O Lord.

All:

Jesus, we believe in you, we hope in you, we love you. Through your cross you brought us the hope of resurrection.

V

John 19:28

When Jesus knew that all was now finished, he said (in order to fulfill the scripture),

All:

"I am thirsty."

Silent prayer, reflective music, or meditative comment may follow.

Leader:

Have mercy on us, O Lord.

All:

Jesus, we believe in you, we hope in you, we love you. Through your cross you brought us the hope of resurrection.

VI

John 19:29–30

A jar full of sour wine was standing there. So they put a sponge full of the wine on a branch of hyssop and held it to his mouth. When Jesus had received the wine, he said,

All:

"It is finished."

Silent prayer, reflective music, or meditative comment may follow.

Leader:

Have mercy on us, O Lord.

All:

Jesus, we believe in you, we hope in you, we love you. Through your cross you brought us the hope of resurrection.

VII

Luke 23:44–46

It was now about noon, and darkness came over the whole land until three in the afternoon, while the sun's light failed; and the curtain of the temple was torn in two. Then Jesus, crying with a loud voice, said,

All:

"Father, into your hands I commend my spirit."

Silent prayer, reflective music, or meditative comment may follow.

Leader:

Have mercy on us, O Lord.

All:

Jesus, we believe in you, we hope in you, we love you. Through your cross you brought us the hope of resurrection.

LITANY

Response:

Lord, save your people.

DISMISSAL

Leader:

"I will not leave you orphaned; I am coming to you."

John 14:18

All:

Holy God, mighty God, ever-living God, have mercy on us.

Leader:

Go in peace to serve the Lord in one another.

All:

Thanks be to God.

The prayer service may conclude with an appropriate song.

Blessing of Foods at Easter

Call to Worship

Leader:
May the grace and peace of Jesus Christ be with you.

All:
And also with you.

Leader:
Friends, let us be attentive to the word of God.

Reading of the Word of God

First Reading
Deuteronomy 26:1–5a, 10–11

Response
Psalm 145

Leader:
I will extol you, my God and King,
    and bless your name forever and ever.
Every day I will bless you,
    and praise your name forever and ever.
Great is the LORD, and greatly to be praised;
    his greatness is unsearchable.

All:
**One generation shall laud your works
    to another,
    and shall declare your mighty acts.
On the glorious splendor of your majesty,
    and on your wondrous works,
      I will meditate.**

Leader:
The might of your awesome deeds
    shall be proclaimed,
    and I will declare your greatness.
They shall celebrate the fame of your
    abundant goodness,
    and shall sing aloud of your righteousness.

All:
**The LORD is gracious and merciful,
    slow to anger and abounding
      in steadfast love.
The LORD is good to all,
    and his compassion is over all
      that he has made.**

Leader:
All your works shall give thanks to you,
    O LORD,
    and all your faithful shall bless you.
They shall speak of the glory of your kingdom,
    and tell of your power,
to make known to all people
    your mighty deeds,
    and the glorious splendor of your kingdom.

All:
**Your kingdom is an everlasting kingdom,
    and your dominion endures
      throughout all generations.
The LORD is faithful in all his words,
    and gracious in all his deeds.**

Gospel
Matthew 7:7

Blessing of the Paschal Lamb

Blessing of Other Meats

Blessing of Bread

Blessing of Dairy Foods

Blessing of Eggs

Blessing of Cakes and Pastries

Blessing of Other Foods

Blessing of Wine

Blessing of Children and Their Easter Baskets

The leader may sprinkle the foods and people with holy water.

CONCLUDING RITE

Leader:
This is the day the Lord has made.

All:
Let us rejoice and be glad.

Leader:
By faith we rose with Jesus in baptism.

All:
May we remain united with him forever.

Leader:
Go now in peace and may God bless you always.

All:
Amen.

The prayer service may conclude with an appropriate song.

CROWNING AN IMAGE OF THE BLESSED VIRGIN MARY

The prayer service may begin with an appropriate song.

OPENING PRAYER

READING OF THE WORD OF GOD

Acts 1:12–14

Response

Leader:
Mary gives us Jesus, the light of the world.

All:
May he shine forth through us.

Leader:
Mary gives us Jesus crucified.

All:
May we die to our selfish inclinations.

Leader:
Mary gives us Jesus, risen to new life.

All:
May we rise with him to eternal glory.

Any appropriate Marian hymn may be sung.
The crowning may occur during the hymn.

LITANY OF MARY,
MOTHER OF THE CHURCH

Leader:
Lord, have mercy.

All:
Lord, have mercy.

Leader:
Christ, have mercy.

All:
Christ, have mercy.

Leader:
Lord, have mercy.

All:
Lord, have mercy.

Leader:
God our Father in heaven,

All:
Have mercy on us.

Leader:
God the Son, our Redeemer,

All:
Have mercy on us.

Leader:
God the Holy Spirit,

All:
Have mercy on us.

Leader:
Holy Trinity, one God,

All:
Have mercy on us.

Leader:
Please respond "Pray for us" after each invocation.
Holy Mary,

All:
R/. Pray for us.

Leader:
Mother of God, **R/.**
Woman of faith, **R/.**
Most honored of all virgins, **R/.**
Joy of Israel, **R/.**
Honor of our people, **R/.**
Model of prayer and virtue, **R/.**
Incentive to trust, **R/.**
Temple of the Holy Spirit, **R/.**
Spouse of Joseph, **R/.**
Mother of Jesus, **R/.**
Faithful follower of Jesus, **R/.**
Mother of the Church, **R/.**
Image of the Church at prayer, **R/.**
Our Lady of Guadalupe, patroness of
    the Americas, **R/.**
Mary Immaculate, patroness of the
    United States, **R/.**
Advocate of life, **R/.**
Guide of the young, **R/.**
Friend of the single, **R/.**
Companion of the married, **R/.**

Voice for the unborn, **R/.**
Mother of mothers, **R/.**
Support of the family, **R/.**
Comforter of the sick, **R/.**
Nurse of the aged, **R/.**
Echo of the suffering, **R/.**
Consoler of the widowed, **R/.**
Strength of the brokenhearted, **R/.**
Hymn of the joyful, **R/.**
Hope of the poor, **R/.**
Example of detachment for the rich, **R/.**
Goal of pilgrims, **R/.**
Resort of the traveler, **R/.**
Protector of the exiled, **R/.**
Woman most whole, **R/.**
Virgin most free, **R/.**
Wife most loving, **R/.**
Mother most fulfilled, **R/.**
Queen of love, **R/.**

Leader:
Lamb of God, you take away the sins of the world:

All:
Have mercy on us.

Leader:
Lamb of God, you take away the sins of the world:

All:
Have mercy on us.

Leader:
Lamb of God, you take away the sins of the world:

All:
Have mercy on us.

All:
Remember, O most loving Virgin Mary,
that never was it known
that anyone who fled to your protection,
implored your help, or sought your intercession
was left unaided.
Inspired with this confidence, we turn to you,
O Virgin of virgins, our Mother.
To you we come, before you we stand,
sinful and sorrowful.
O Mother of the Word Incarnate,
do not despise our petitions,
but in your mercy hear and answer us. Amen.

BLESSING

The prayer service may conclude with an appropriate song.

BLESSING OF PETS

The prayer service may begin with an appropriate song.

OPENING PRAYER

READING OF THE WORD OF GOD

Genesis 2:18–19

INTERCESSIONS

Leader:

Let our response to these prayers be
"Blessed be God forever."

Blessed be God, who created the world and
found it very good. **R/.**

Blessed be God, who formed us out of the clay
of the ground. **R/.**

Blessed be God, who created the animals to be
our helpers. **R/.**

Blessed be God, who created horses, ponies,
and donkeys. **R/.**

Blessed be God, who created poodles and pugs,
beagles and bloodhounds, Dalmatians and
dachshunds, and dogs of every mixed breed. **R/.**

Blessed be God, who created Siamese and
Burmese, tabbies and tortoiseshells, Manx and
Maine coons, and cats of every size and color. **R/.**

Blessed be God, who created hamsters and
gerbils, ferrets and guinea pigs, rabbits and
mice, and every kind of small pet. **R/.**

Blessed be God, who created parrots and
parakeets, canaries and cockatoos, finches and
pheasants, and every kind of tamed and wild
bird. **R/.**

Blessed be God, who created frogs and toads,
lizards and turtles, snakes and salamanders, and
every kind of amphibian and reptile. **R/.**

Blessed be God, who created goldfish and
angelfish, koi and clownfish, tetras and trout,
and every kind of fish that swims in the seas,
rivers, lakes, and aquariums. **R/.**

Blessed be God, who created pot-belly pigs and
pinto ponies, owls and ocelots, alligators and
anteaters, and every kind of unusual pet. **R/.**

Blessed be God, who created every kind of
animal, and found them very good. **R/.**

BLESSING PRAYER

Leader:

God our Creator, you made all things good.
In love look now on us and on our pets
and on all the creatures you have made.
As you once sent your angel Raphael
to guide your servant Tobiah
   and his faithful dog,
send your angel to watch over our pets.
Keep them in health and safety,
   secure in our care
to be our comfort and joy.
Remember them for life,
for you delight in life.
We ask this through Christ our Lord.

*The leader may then ask that each pet be brought forward for an
individual blessing, or may sprinkle the pets with blessed water.*

CONCLUDING RITE

The prayer service may conclude with an appropriate song.

A VIGIL SERVICE BEFORE CHRISTMAS

This service can suitably close the Advent season or be used as a prelude to one of the Masses of the Vigil of Christmas.

The prayer service may begin with an appropriate song.

I

THE GREAT "O" ANTIPHONS

Leader:
During these past weeks we have been preparing to celebrate the Lord's coming. Today we know that he will come and in the morning we will see his glory. Now we recall the long centuries during which humanity longed for salvation. We relive that expectation as we sing an ancient Advent song.

Leader:
Jesus is Emmanuel, "God with us," promised when our first parents became exiles from God and captives of sin. Because we desire him among us, we sing: "O come, O come, Emmanuel!"

Song: *O Come, O Come, Emmanuel*, verse 1

Leader:
Jesus is the Word of God and Wisdom of the Father for all eternity. We sing the praises of the one who existed before the world began: "Come, O Wisdom!"

Song: *O Come, O Come, Emmanuel*, verse 2

Leader:
The Lord of might appeared in the flames of the burning bush on Mount Sinai. We ask God to make us worthy to enter the Promised Land. We cry out: "Come, O Lord of might."

Song: *O Come, O Come, Emmanuel*, verse 3

Leader:
Jesus is the flower of Jesse's stem. No greater flower bloomed on the family tree of Jesse, King David's father. Jesus would become the tree of life that brings us salvation, and so we pray: "Come, O Branch of Jesse's stem!"

Song: *O Come, O Come, Emmanuel*, verse 4

Leader:
Jesus is the key of David. He came to unlock the prison of death and release us from the bonds of sin. We are grateful that he gave us freedom as we sing: "Come, O Key of David!"

Song: *O Come, O Come, Emmanuel*, verse 5

Leader:
Jesus is the daystar, the sun that brightens the world's darkness. We will see him in splendor when he comes again. On that day he will cheer us, and so we sing: "Come, O Daystar!"

Song: *O Come, O Come, Emmanuel*, verse 6

Leader:
Jesus is the Desired One of the nations, who unites us into one family. He was foretold as King and Prince of Peace. We his people sing: "O Come, Desire of Nations!"

Song: *O Come, O Come, Emmanuel*, verse 7

A choral/congregational program of carols may follow, and the service may conclude with the Posada procession.

II

THE POSADA PROCESSION
The crib scene has been prepared without the figures of Jesus, Mary, and Joseph. It is now illuminated. The following ceremony is based on the Hispanic custom of the posada (inn) procession searching for a place of shelter and rest.

Leader:
During the past weeks we have been preparing to celebrate the Lord's coming. Today we know that he will come and in the morning we shall see his glory.

Song: *O Little Town of Bethlehem*, verse 1
The presiding minister and other ministers go in procession to a side entrance of the church. After the first verse there is silence, and a knock is sounded at that door. A person there may engage in this dialogue with the people:

Joseph:

In the name of heaven, good friends, give us a place to stay this night.

All:

This is not an inn; keep going. We don't open to strangers.

Song: *O Little Town of Bethlehem*, verse 2
During the song's second verse, the procession moves to another side entrance. The knocking occurs again, followed by this dialogue:

Joseph:

I am Joseph, the carpenter from Nazareth. Do not refuse us, that God may reward you.

All:

We don't care who you are; let us sleep. We already told you we won't let you in.

Song: *O Little Town of Bethlehem*, verse 3
During the third verse, the procession moves to the main entrance. The knocking occurs again, followed by this dialogue:

Joseph:

My beloved wife, Mary, can go no farther. She is heaven's Queen who will bear God's Son.

All:

Enter, holy pilgrims; you may use this poor place. Our houses and our hearts are open to you.

Song: *O Little Town of Bethlehem*, verse 4
The presiding minister opens the door to admit Mary and Joseph. During the singing of the fourth verse, representatives of parish organizations or children accompany the procession to the crib scene, carrying the figures of Jesus, Mary, and Joseph for placement there.

Song: *Silent Night* or *O Come, Little Children* or any appropriate song

The Christmas crib may be blessed at this time.

PRAYER SERVICE BEFORE ELECTIONS

The prayer service may begin with an appropriate song.

CALL TO WORSHIP

Leader:
O God, open our eyes,

All:
That we may see the way of truth.

Leader:
O Lord, keep us from all selfish intent,

All:
And hear us when we call on you.

OPENING PRAYER

READING OF THE WORD OF GOD

First Reading
Exodus 18:20–22, 24; Deuteronomy 1:16–17

Response
Psalm 72:1–2, 3–4ab, 7–8, 12–13, 17

Leader:
In his days may righteousness flourish
and peace abound, until the moon is no more.

All:
**In his days may righteousness flourish
and peace abound, until the moon is no more.**

Leader:
Give the king your justice, O God,
and your righteousness to a king's son.
May he judge your people with righteousness,
and your poor with justice.

All:
**May the mountains yield prosperity
for the people,
and the hills, in righteousness.
May he defend the cause of the poor
of the people,
give deliverance to the needy,
and crush the oppressor.**

Leader:
In his days may righteousness flourish,
and peace abound until the moon is no more.
May he have dominion from sea to sea,
and from the River to the ends of the earth.

All:
**For he delivers the needy when they call,
the poor and those who have no helper.
He has pity on the weak and the needy,
and saves the lives of the needy.**

Leader:
May his name endure forever,
his fame continue as long as the sun.
May all nations be blessed in him;
may they pronounce him happy.

Second Reading
2 Chronicles 19:4–6; 9

INTERCESSIONS

Leader:
We conclude our service with prayer for God's help.

That love for justice may prevail in our elections, we pray to the Lord.

All:
R/. Lord, hear us and lead us to justice.

CONCLUSION

Leader:
The peace of God be with us. May God guide our deliberations with the light of holy wisdom as we decide on suitable representatives in government.

All:
Thanks be to God.

The prayer service may conclude with an appropriate song.

PRAYER SERVICE
FOR INDEPENDENCE DAY

The prayer service may begin with an appropriate song.

OPENING PRAYER

READING OF THE WORD OF GOD

Psalm 9:1–2, 9–10

Response
America the Beautiful or any appropriate song

Second Reading
Isaiah 32:16–18

Response (inspired by Abraham Lincoln's
Second Inaugural Address)

Leader:
With malice toward none, with charity for all,

All:
R/. The fruit of righteousness is sown in peace.

Leader:
With firmness in the right, as God gives us to
see the right, **R/.**

Leader:
Let us strive to finish the work we are in,
to bind up the nation's wounds, **R/.**

Leader:
To care for him who shall have borne the battle
and his widow and orphan, **R/.**

Leader:
To do all which may achieve and cherish a just
and lasting peace among ourselves and with all
nations, **R/.**

*A public leader may address the assembly. In lieu of an address there
may be some other manifestation of civic pride, such as a fireworks
display where authorized, a patriotic musical performance, an
artillery salute, or the raising or posting of the flag.*

RESOLUTION

Leader:
Will you foster peace within our country
and good will among all people?

All:
We will.

Leader:
Will you stand up for justice by keeping our laws
and fulfilling the divine law of love?

All:
We will.

Leader:
Will you labor to enrich our land with your
God-given talents, curing its ills and cherishing
life in all its forms?

All:
We will.

LITANY OF PETITION

Leader:
Let us pray for our country,
that it may be a blessing to the world.
Let our response be "Lord, hear our prayer."

CLOSING PRAYER

DISMISSAL

Leader:
Go forth in peace and freedom, renewed in
spirit to make our promised land of yesteryear
a true home for today and a sanctuary for all
future generations.

All:
Amen.

The prayer service may conclude with an appropriate song.

PRAYER SERVICE FOR PEACE BASED ON THE WORDS OF SAINT FRANCIS OF ASSISI

The prayer service may begin with an appropriate song.

CALL TO WORSHIP

Leader:
Blessed are the peacemakers;
for they will be called children of God.

Matthew 5:9

All:
Lord, make me an instrument of your peace.

OPENING PRAYER

READING OF THE WORD OF GOD

First Reading
Isaiah 2:1–5

Response
Psalm 122:6–8

All:
Pray for the peace of Jerusalem:
**   "May they prosper who love you.**
Peace be within your walls,
**   and security within your towers."**
For the sake of my relatives and friends
**   I will say, "Peace be within you."**

Second Reading
Philippians 4:6–9

Response
Colossians 1:19–20

All:
In Christ Jesus all the fullness of God
was pleased to dwell,
and through him God was pleased
to reconcile to himself all things,
whether on earth or in heaven,
by making peace through the blood
of his cross.

RESOLUTION

Leader:
Peace I leave with you;
    my peace I give to you.

John 14:27

All:
Lord, make me an instrument of your peace.

Leader:
Do not be overcome by evil,
    but overcome evil with good.

Romans 12:21

All:
Where there is hatred, let me sow love.

Leader:
Father, forgive them;
    for they do not know what they are doing.

Luke 23:34

All:
Where there is injury, let me sow pardon.

Leader:
Do not doubt but believe.

John 20:27

All:
Where there is doubt, let me sow faith.

Leader:
Hope does not disappoint us, because God's
love has been poured into our hearts through
the Holy Spirit that has been given to us.

Romans 5:5

All:
Where there is despair, let me sow hope.

Leader:
You are the light of the world. In the same way,
let your light shine before others, so that they
may see your good works and give glory to your
Father in heaven.

Matthew 5:14, 16

All:
Where there is darkness, let me sow light.

Leader:
You will weep and mourn, but the world will
rejoice; you will have pain, but your pain will
turn into joy.

John 16:20

All:

Where there is sadness, let me sow joy.

Leader:

God consoles us in all our affliction, so that we may be able to console those who are in any affliction with the consolation with which we ourselves are consoled by God.

2 Corinthians 1:4

All:

Divine Master, grant that I may not so much seek to be consoled as to console.

Leader:

With all wisdom and insight he has made known to us the mystery of his will, according to his good pleasure that he set forth in Christ.

Ephesians 1:8–9

All:

Grant that I may not so much seek to be understood as to understand.

Leader:

If I speak in the tongues of mortals and of angels, but do not have love, I am a noisy gong or a clanging cymbal.

1 Corinthians 13:1

All:

Grant that I may not so much seek to be loved as to love.

Leader:

For those who want to save their life will lose it, and those who lose their life for my sake will save it.

Luke 9:24

All:

It is in giving that we receive.

Leader:

Forgive us our debts as we also have forgiven our debtors.

Mark 6:12

All:

It is in pardoning that we are pardoned.

Leader:

Unless a grain of wheat falls into the earth and dies, it remains just a single grain; but if it dies, it bears much fruit.

John 12:24

All:

It is in dying that we are born to eternal life.

BLESSING

Leader:

May God the Father and the Lord Jesus Christ grant us peace, love, and faith.

All:

Grace be with all who love our Lord Jesus Christ with unfailing love.

The prayer service may conclude with an appropriate song.

PRAYER SERVICES FOR PARISH LIFE © 2004, World Library Publications • 800-566-6150 • WLP 017264. Scripture quotations are from the New Revised Standard Version of the Bible © 1989 by the Division of Christian Education of the National Council of the Churches of Christ in the USA. All rights reserved. Used with permission.

SERVICE OF PRAYER FOR PEACE

The prayer service may begin with an appropriate song.

GREETING

Leader:
In the name of the Father, and of the Son, and of the Holy Spirit.

All:
Amen.

Leader:
May abundant grace and the abiding peace of God be with you all.

All:
And also with you.

OPENING PRAYER

READING OF THE WORD OF GOD

First Reading
Isaiah 11:1–10

Response
Psalm 72:1–7, 12–14

Leader:
In his days may righteousness flourish
   and peace abound, until the moon
     is no more.

All:
Give the king your justice, O God,
   and your righteousness to a king's son.
May he judge your people
    with righteousness,
   and your poor with justice.

Leader:
May the mountains yield prosperity
    for the people,
   and the hills, in righteousness.
May he defend the cause of the poor
    of the people,
   give deliverance to the needy,
   and crush the oppressor.

All:
May he live while the sun endures,
   and as long as the moon,
    throughout all generations.
May he be like rain that falls
   on the mown grass,
   like showers that water the earth.

Leader:
For he delivers the needy when they call,
   the poor and those who have no helper.
He has pity on the weak and the needy,
   and saves the lives of the needy.

All:
From oppression and violence he redeems
   their life;
   and precious is their blood in his sight.
In his days may righteousness flourish
   and peace abound, until the moon
    is no more.

Gospel
John 20:19–23

INTERCESSIONS

LORD'S PRAYER

CLOSING PRAYER

BLESSING AND DISMISSAL

The prayer service may conclude with an appropriate song.

Prayer Service for Comfort in Time of Disaster

The prayer service may begin with an appropriate song.

Opening Prayer

Reading of the Word of God

First Reading
Lamentations 3:17–26

or

Romans 8:31b–39

Response
Psalm 80:1–7, 14–19

Leader:
Give ear, O Shepherd of Israel,
   you who lead Joseph like a flock!
You who are enthroned upon the cherubim,
     shine forth
     before Ephraim and Benjamin
       and Manasseh.
Stir up your might,
   and come and save us!

All:
**Stir up your might,
   and come and save us!
Restore us, O God;
   let your face shine, that we may be saved.**

Leader:
Restore us, O God;
   let your face shine, that we may be saved.
O Lord God of hosts,
   how long will you be angry
      with your people's prayers?
You have fed them with the bread of tears,
   and given them tears to drink
      in full measure.

All:
**You have fed them with the bread of tears,
   and given them tears to drink
      in full measure.
You make us the scorn of our neighbors;
   our enemies laugh among themselves.
Restore us, O God of hosts;
   let your face shine, that we may be saved.**

Leader:
Restore us, O God of hosts;
   let your face shine, that we may be saved.
Turn again, O God of hosts;
   look down from heaven, and see;
have regard for this vine,
   the stock that your right hand has planted.
They have burned it with fire,
      they have cut it down;
   may they perish at the rebuke
      of your countenance.

All:
**They have burned it with fire,
      they have cut it down;
   may they perish at the rebuke
      of your countenance.
But let your hand be upon the one
      at your right hand,
   the one whom you made strong
      for yourself.
Then we will never turn back from you;
   give us life, and we will call on your name.
Restore us, O Lord God of hosts;
   let your face shine, that we may be saved.**

Gospel
John 11:17–28

Intercessions

Leader:
Like Martha in today's Gospel, we often entreat
God, crying, "What if?" and "If only." Let us
cry out to God now on behalf of all who have
been affected by the tragedy of recent days.

O God, you are the giver of life;

All:
Grant eternal life to those who have died.

Leader:
O God, you are the source of all truth;

All:
Help us to know the truth of your care for us.

Leader:
O God, you are the wellspring of healing;

All:
Bring comfort and strength to all who have been injured.

Leader:
O God, you are the fountain of consolation;

All:
Console those who have lost loved ones.

Leader:
O God, you alone have power over evil;

All:
Lead all who would harm your people to a change of heart.

Leader:
O God, you are Lord of heaven and earth;

All:
Hear us in our need and answer our prayer.

LORD'S PRAYER

CLOSING PRAYER

SIGN OF PEACE

The prayer service may conclude with an appropriate song.

CD-ROM INFORMATION

The CD-ROM that accompanies this book contains the leaders' and people's versions of each of the prayer services found herein. You will need the Adobe® Reader® in order to read and print these files. If you do not yet have it installed on your system, visit www.adobe.com to obtain a free download of the Adobe® Reader®.

FINDING THE FILES ON THE CD

There are eight folders on the CD, which correspond to the headings in this book's Table of Contents. Within each folder are the prayer services that are found under that heading. To open a prayer service, double-click on its associated folder, then double-click on the prayer service that you want to see. It should open in the Adobe® Reader® application on your hard drive. You can now view and print as much of that prayer service as you need. Please note that several people's versions consist of two pages.